Vehicule Days

An Unorthodox History of Montreal's Vehicule Poets

edited by Ken Norris

Published with the assistance of The Canada Council
and the Québec Ministry of Culture.
Printed and bound in Canada by Les Ateliers Graphiques Marc Veilleux.
Dépôt légal, Bibliothèque nationale du Québec and the National Library of Canada.

Canadian Cataloguing in Publication Data

Main entry under title:

Vehicule Days : an unorthodox history of Montréal's Vehicule Poets

ISBN 0-921833-11-3

1. Canadian poetry (English) - - Québec (Province) - - Montréal - - History and criticism. 2. Canadian poetry (English) - - 20th century- - History and criticism. I. Norris, Ken, 1951- .

PS8159.7.M6V44 1993 C811'.5409 C93-090639-X
PR9190.5.V44 1993

NuAge Editions, P.O. Box 8, Station E, Montréal, Québec, H2T 3A5

Table of Contents

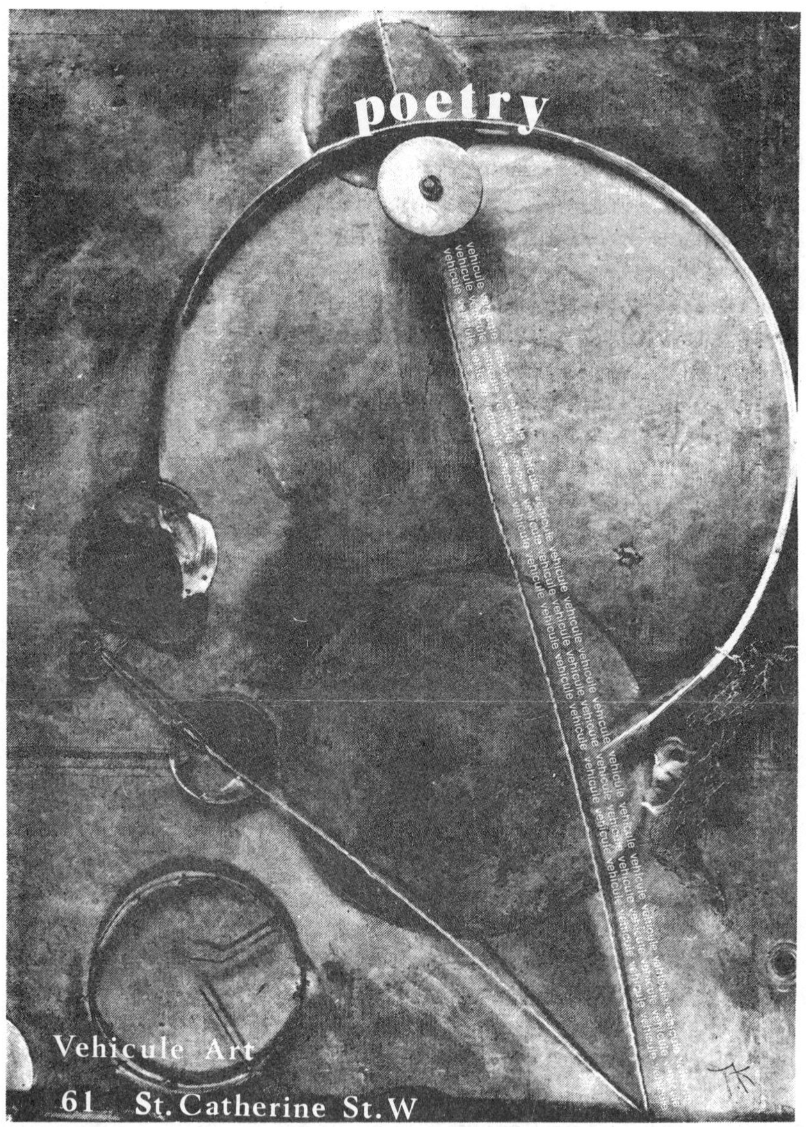

sundays at two

Oct. 2. Anne McLean

Oct. 9. Barry McKinnon

Oct. 16. Four Vermont Poets

Oct. 23. Claude Beausoleil & Yolande Villemaire

Oct. 30. Claudia Lapp

Nov. 6. Film – Blood of the Poet Jean Cocteau (1929)

Nov. 13. Al Purdy

Nov. 20. Open Reading

Nov. 27. F.R. Scott

Dec. 4. Poetry On Tape

Dec. 11. Martin Newman & Ray Filip

Introduction

In the beginning there was one Véhicule: Véhicule Art (Inc.), a parallel gallery, located at 61 Ste. Catherine Street West. Founded by thirteen young visual artists, the gallery opened its doors as an exhibition space in October of 1972, hoping to provide experimental artists with a venue denied to them by the commercial galleries. In December of that year the gallery also hosted the first of many Sunday afternoon poetry readings, giving impetus to a renaissance in Montreal poetry and to the Vehicule Poets movement in particular. In a back room of the gallery a printing press was installed (initially to print up publicity flyers and posters for the gallery), giving birth shortly thereafter to a printing cooperative which, with time, came to be known as Véhicule Press. The gallery, poets, and press all shared a space and time and cultural commitment which revolutionized the Montreal cultural scene. Had the gallery never opened in 1972, the cultural community of Montreal would now be much poorer on a number of fronts.

A decade later, what had once been one Véhicule had splintered into three or four separate entities. Véhicule Art (Inc.) had become La Musée d'art vivant Véhicule, which inhabited a more trendy space up the street at 307 Ste. Catherine Street West. Prime Video (Véhicule's video division) had split off from the gallery, leaving the exhibition space to the visual artists. The press had moved out of the original gallery space in 1977 and set up shop in Chinatown. The Vehicule poets had abandoned the gallery, severed their editorial ties with the press, and held a "Last of the Vehicule Poets" reading at Concordia University in 1981. When the gallery closed its doors in June of 1982, it confirmed the death of the concepts of community and collectivity that had been at the very core of Véhicule.

With these shared origins in mind, this book takes as its subject the (unorthodox) history of the Vehicule Poets (hopefully we will see discrete studies of both Véhicule Art and Véhicule Press in the not-so-distant future). These seven writers—Endre Farkas, Artie Gold, Tom Konyves, Claudia Lapp, John McAuley, Stephen Morrissey and Ken Norris—were all involved with the operations of the gallery—a number of them serving on the gallery executive—and all published books with Véhicule Press circa 1973-80. Three of them—Farkas, Gold and Norris—served as the Véhicule Press editorial board from 1975-81. In 1979, they published a collective anthology, *The Vehicule Poets*, with McAuley's Maker Press (deciding to forego the accent on the "e" of "Véhicule" because they were a group of poets who wrote in English).

What initially brought the Vehicule Poets together, beyond the proximity of the gallery, is that they shared an interest in hip American poetry and experimental European art movements. Their poetic tastes were certainly individual and eclectic, but they took great interest in introducing one another to their own specific poetic enthusiasms. Looking out onto the Canadian literary scene, the poetry that made the most sense to them was being published by the Coach House-Talonbooks nexus, which built upon the innovations of the *Tish* group and experimental poets such as bill bissett, Gerry Gilbert and bpNichol. In emulating these proponents of literary community and poetic experimentation (two ideas which ran counter to the rather conservative literary trends in Montreal at the time), the Vehicule Poets bonded together to form the most cohesive poetry movement in Canada since the *Tish* days of the early 1960s.

As young writers, all of the Vehicule Poets were very much concerned with standard writerly issues, among them being the gaining of access to the means of production. The members of the group produced a number of little magazines (among them Morrissey's *what is* and *Montreal Journal of Poetics*, McAuley's *Maker*, Konyves' *Hh*, Norris' *CrossCountry* and *Every Man His Own Football*, and the collective *mouse eggs*. This magazine activity enabled them to establish contact with other writers and gave them a forum for their initial poetical works; at a later stage, it enabled them to give an airing to work that did not feed into mainstream taste. Their ready access to Véhicule Press, CrossCountry Press and Maker Press enabled them to produce their early books without much outside editorial interference. Relying upon one another for guidance and feedback, they produced their early books in a spirit of collectivity and collaboration. This collective spirit is very much in evidence in the early published work.

As a number of the Vehicule Poets suggest in various texts within this book, the gallery left an indelible mark of its own upon them. Exposure to what was going on at the cutting edge of visual arts, video and performance art led many of the Vehicule Poets to think beyond the page when it came to their own work. The poets first encountered the gallery as a reading space, which they utilized on Sunday afternoons; but it very quickly became for them an "artistic atmosphere" that was always in flux and was constantly challenging them. As the gallery "internationalized" its exhibition schedules, and the poets became more involved in the everyday operations of the gallery, the inspirations for their poetry became blindingly diverse. By 1977, a number of the Vehicule Poets had started to move into videopoetry (Konyves' term) and poetry performance.

An initial concern for "documenting" poetry readings had yielded to a growing interest in mixed media and performance art. While Véhicule Press produced books of their more conventional texts, it was within the gallery space that the Vehicule Poets presented simultaneous readings, poetry and dance performances, poetry and music performances, video installations, and mounted exhibitions of concrete poetry. Eventually feeling somewhat constrained by the friendly confines of the gallery, they went on in the late seventies to put poetry on Montreal's city buses (*poésie en mouvement*), visual and performance art on Montreal's cable channel (*Art Montréal*), and even performed Pound's "In a Station of the Metro" in Montreal's metro system. A number of them recorded an album of experimental sound texts in 1980 (*Sounds Like*). Several of the Vehicule Poets organized road tours for poetry performances which they took out to parallel galleries and other arts centers across the country.

As with their magazine and book activities, a number of the cultural and performance projects the Vehicule Poets undertook had collective and collaborative origins. They worked in consultation with one another on the cultural projects, and often collaborated in the writing of performance and video pieces (sometimes also serving as stagehands and bit players). This was a modus operandi that served them well for a number of years.

However, as with many other artistic and literary movements, as they developed as writers they began to pursue their own individual initiatives more and more. By the early 1980s their collaborations were few and far between (and certainly not without friction). It was at this time that the group was officially dissolved. The motivation for a public dissolution of the movement was the logical recognition that after the group comes the individual, that, as the Vehicule Poets, they had done as much as they could do.

In offering this history of the Vehicule Poets, I've tried to come at their "historical moment" from a variety of angles. Perhaps one of the most curious angles is that this book is edited by someone who was a card-carrying member of the Vehicule Poets. So much for cool objectivity (but perhaps as a culture we are done with that fiction anyway). Beyond this introduction, however, the book has no other editorial apparatus, and I have tried to let the material contained speak for itself. It is my hope that the book combines the best qualities of "document," "documentation," and "oral history."

The book's first section is essentially a collection of documents, poetry and poetics essays from the "Véhicule days." The three initial articles offer an argument between critic David O'Rourke and me which gives a sense of the poetic environment in Montreal at the time, and perhaps reveal what everyone thought was at stake (while also recalling earlier literary debates like the *Preview-First Statement* antagonism of three decades earlier). Artie Gold's introduction to *The Vehicule Poets* accompanies a selection of work excerpted from that anthology, offering the reader a sampling of what the poets were up to on the page at the time.

A Real Good Goosin': Talking Poetics reveals the Vehicule Poets *not* cracking under interrogation by Louis Dudek; instead, an interesting discussion of postmodern poetics ensues. The balance of the section consists of poetics essays written by individual authors, almost all of which made their initial appearance in Stephen Morrissey's important *Montreal Journal of Poetics*.

The second section of the book consists of retrospectives and interviews which reflect back upon the "Véhicule days." An older and wiser George Bowering, often cited as a significant "mentor" of the Vehicule Poets, reflects on how he taught several of them "creative writhing" at Sir George Williams University. Claudia Lapp, in an essay from which the book takes its title, tells us of how "Montreal has always been my poetic home and Vehicule my 'tribe.'" In interview, Konyves, Farkas, Morrissey and Norris try to make sense of their "Véhicule experiences," while also offering insight into their later development as poets.

The book's concluding section offers an intriguing sampling of new work from each of the seven Vehicule Poets, now all in their forties.

In this book I've tried to present a number of significant visual documents that amplify the print documentation of the Vehicule Poets. Much of the activities of the Vehicule Poets that took place beyond the bounds of printed books have been invisible for a number of years. In his *Poetry in Performance*, Tom Konyves was the only Vehicule Poet who ever attempted to put into book form examples of videopoetry, videotheatre and performance poetry. Much of the mixed media work that was done at the time has gone undocumented. I'm hopeful that these reproductions of posters, photographs and texts will help to round out a sense of the atmosphere of those ground-breaking Véhicule days.

Ken Norris
Bangor, Maine
July 19, 1993

PROVERBSI #68

Moderation is the father of death.

Montreal English Poetry in the Seventies

Ken Norris

CVII 3:3, January 1978

English poetry in Montreal has always been written under unique conditions. Living as a member of a minority culture within the bounds of a dominant French culture has made the poet in Montreal intensely aware of his own language as well as informing him as to the problems inherent in the use of language as an agent of communication. When he writes a poem, the Montreal poet knows of the limited access he has to an audience. The vast majority of people living in the same city as the one he inhabits have no interest whatsoever in what he has to say because what he is saying is in a language that has no relevance to their inner life. The Montreal poet also recognizes that, as a Quebecois, he is isolated from the rest of English Canada and that there is not an open line of communication running between himself and it. To write poetry in English in Montreal is to produce something that it seems next to no one wants. Yet, despite this somewhat sobering fact, or possibly because of it, Montreal has served as one of the centers of English poetry for most of this century and is currently beginning again to assert itself after the lull it experienced during the late sixties. Louis Dudek has written "It is the destiny of Montreal to show the country from time to time what poetry is"; that is a statement few Montreal poets would disagree with; they take their craft seriously, writing as they do in a language that is, in many ways, under siege. The history of English poetry in Montreal is a long one, and it is one that shows no signs of terminating. Montreal in the seventies is a city that is vitally alive with poetry.

It was with the final folding of the little magazine *Intercourse* in 1973 that the disjointed Montreal poetry scene of the 60s came to its end and made room for the new movement. This event marked the end of an era that began in 1956 with the inception of the magazine *Yes*, edited by John Lachs, Glen Siebrasse and Michael Gnarowski, and the publication of Leonard Cohen's first book, *Let Us Compare Mythologies*, by Louis Dudek as the first volume in the McGill Poetry Series. The 60s were an interesting time in Montreal, for it was the time that Montreal lost the poetic spotlight it held for over 30 years to the Vancouver *Tish* poets and other manifestations of New Wave Canada.

Montreal had held the historical spotlight since November of 1925 when F.R. Scott and A.J.M. Smith took part in the founding of *The McGill Fortnightly Review*, and in so doing, launched the McGill Movement which played a major part in bringing modernism to Canada. The spirit of modernism which they infused into Canadian poetry in the

1920s tentatively continued to manifest itself through the Depression years when poetry publication was sparse and there was not a significant little magazine dedicated to the cause of modernism in all of Canada. In the early 40s, the literary feud between *Preview* and *First Statement* sparked the fires of social realism which burned bright in Montreal at that time, bringing to light poets such as Louis Dudek, Irving Layton, Raymond Souster, (based in Toronto, but an active member of this group), P.K. Page and Miriam Waddington. When this movement faltered after *Preview* and *First Statement* merged into *Northern Review*, edited by John Sutherland, there ensued a lull of several years until Dudek and Layton encouraged Souster in his publication of *Contact* and helped Aileen Collins to start *CIV/n*, both magazines making further inroads in the modernist cause; these publications worked counter to what *Northern Review* was doing at the time, captained by Sutherland's increasingly Catholic taste. One can see that there was a substantial poetic tradition of social realism which the editors of *Yes* were quite willing to embrace.

During the mid-fifties there were two growing poetic personalities to be reckoned with: Irving Layton and Leonard Cohen. At this time Layton was just beginning to hit his stride in terms of discovering a truly confident poetic voice, finding acceptance with the critics who had earlier panned his work (most notable of these being Northrop Frye), and learning how to attract media attention. Almost simultaneously, Leonard Cohen emerged in full bloom out of the halls of McGill University, already showing signs of the sardonic black romanticism that would come to full realization in his later poetry and songs.

It was between the pillars of Dudek's social realism and Layton's and Cohen's poetry of personality that the Montreal poets of the sixties walked. Continuing in the mode of social realism, they explored the urban realities a bit more extensively than their predecessors; some followed in the footsteps of Layton, Cohen and the older A.M. Klein in exploring the poetry of Jewish tradition, or else followed Layton and Cohen in working in the mode of the poetry of personality. When the Layton-Dudek verbal duels heated up in the early sixties, the editors of *Cataract* (Seymour Mayne, K.V. Hertz, and Leonard Angel) seemingly sided with Layton by publishing some of his attacks upon Dudek. Michael Gnarowski and Glen Siebrasse gravitated towards Dudek and his poetic orientation, finding themselves working in a closer and closer alliance with Dudek until the three of them were jointly running Delta Canada Press.

Most of the Montreal little magazines of the sixties were sporadic, as was the movement of that time. *Cataract* was printed from 1961-1962, eventually superseded for one issue by *Catapult* in 1964. David Rosenfield edited one issue of *The Bloody Horse* in 1963; Seymour

Mayne edited *The Page*, a series of broadsheets, in 1964; K.V. Hertz was later to edit *Ingluvin* for two issues in the early seventies. Although *Yes* operated out of Montreal for most of its fourteen years of existence (1956-1970), it was never a magazine of a new movement; rather it continued to reinforce the inroads of the forties and fifties, never taking a truly fighting stand until its last few issues when it came out in opposition to *Tish* and the new poetic innovations of the sixties, attempting too late to stem the tide of New Wave Canada. Not surprisingly, it posited the poetry of social realism as the alternative.

It was in Dudek's personal magazine *Delta* (1957-1966) that the full panoply of young Montreal poets of the late fifties and early sixties appeared, though never as part of a militant movement. Young Montrealers such as Daryl Hine, Ian Clark, Michael Gnarowski, Milton Acorn and Al Purdy (in Montreal at the time), John Lachs, Lionel Tiger, Sylvia Barnard, Phyllis Webb, George Ellenbogen, Marquita Crevier, Dave Solway, Avi Boxer, Raymond Fraser, Pierre Coupey, Seymour Mayne, Henry Moscovitch, and Steve Smith all appeared within the pages of *Delta*.

The Montreal poetry scene of the sixties was a failure for several reasons. The first of these is that, by and large, it had nothing new to offer in terms of poetics and poetic techniques. At a time when the rest of Canada was being influenced by an influx of various new ideas and experiments in poetry, ranging from Black Mountain to Dada to North American Indian rituals, the Montreal poets ironically chose to conservatively work within an established poetic tradition. Much of what they wrote was an echoing and pale imitation of Dudek, Layton and Cohen; none of the poets could eclipse their lyrical mastery or come close to cultivating more engaging poetic personalities.

Unlike the *Tish* movement, that of Montreal in the sixties was not something sustained. Some poets moved (Purdy and Acorn in the early sixties heading for parts a bit further west, Mayne going to Vancouver in the mid-sixties), one suffered a breakdown, Steve Smith died an early tragic death, and some, after a few years, simply stopped writing. Montreal, in the sixties, lacked a focused movement and clung too rigidly to the poetic values of the past. Poets writing in the west simply had more to offer.

The beginnings of the current Montreal poetry scene, one that is markedly diversified (just as in the sixties Canada was awakened to the possibility of many different kinds of poetry existing simultaneously, so Montreal has now been similarly awakened), can possibly be seen to range back to 1967 when New Wave Canada made its official entrance into Montreal when George Bowering and Margaret Atwood took up teaching positions at Sir George Williams University. Up until that time, students seeking exposure to poetry in the forum of the university had the choice of Louis Dudek at McGill or Irving Layton at Sir George Williams as their teacher and mentor. Atwood taught Victorian literature and did a reading or two before shortly moving on, but it was Bowering who began teaching creative writing classes; into his classes walked present-day poets Ritchie Carson, John McAuley and Tom Konyves, and a former student of the Colorado School of Mines, Artie Gold, who had never thought of writing poetry before but now suddenly began. Dwight Gardiner, now involved with poetry in Vancouver, also passed through Bowering's classes. Bowering awakened them and other students to the new possibilities of poetry. It was also when Bowering was present at Sir George Williams (1967-1971) that the English department there held its extensive reading series (originally instituted by Roy Kiyooka, Wynne Francis, Stan Hoffman, and Howard Fink, all faculty members) which brought in many poets from across Canada and the United States and exposed the young and aspiring Montreal poets to a wide diversity of poetic techniques. Since Bowering's departure, Montreal poet Richard Sommer has taught creative writing at Sir George and graduated a number of Montreal's current crop of poets.

In 1972, two Montreal little magazines that are significant to the new generation of Montreal poetry started publication: *Booster & Blaster*, which lasted for two issues, and *Anthol*, which continues to this day. For the most part, Montreal little magazines no longer function in the fighting manner they did back in the forties and fifties. Because of Montreal's relative isolation from the rest of Canada, magazines in Montreal have, in the past few years, come to exist as survival outlets for Montreal writing. The magazines tend to be open rather than closed to writers with a different orientation who are writing in the city. This does not indicate that there is no disagreement among Montreal poets as to methods of composition; rather, it shows that, above all things, Montreal writers and editors are dedicated to the continuation of poetry being written in English in Montreal.

Although it was not a magazine of high quality, *Booster & Blaster* performed the important function of bringing Montreal writers together and making them aware of each other. Originally spearheaded by Bryan McCarthy and run by a working committee consisting of Raymond Gordy, Glen Siebrasse, Alan Pearson, Carol Leckner, and Artie Gold, it existed as a cooperative, publishing poets resident in Montreal only. The reasoning behind this was expressed in an editorial by Raymond Gordy in the second issue:

> *The Montreal Free Poet, Booster & Blaster* publishes Montreal poets only. There is a reason in this. We are an English-speaking community, physically circumscribed within a larger French-speaking community, but paradoxically, a minority which shares a majority English-speaking consciousness. This is difficult politics and should create a poetry of meaningful content and commitment. Too much poetry in English Canada is a poetry of experiences, a recording without reflection. Here in Quebec that approach is unacceptable. Here, great English-speaking poetry will be written, not only confessional but historical, dealing with Quebec's distinctive and local reality—survival.

The magazine functioned much in the way of a cooperative workshop. Each poet had to pay for the gestetnering of his or her pages of work. At the back of the magazine there was a section in which the contributing poets "boosted" or "blasted" each other's work, trying to provide some perspective on what was being written. As the editors themselves admitted, some of the poetry was good, much was indifferent, and some was quite bad. *Booster & Blaster* was important not because of the writing it contained, but because it attempted to draw together a fragmented and splintered poetic community.

The other little magazine begun that year was *Anthol,* published for the first time in the spring of 1972. Initially, *Anthol* only published Montreal poets. In the past year the magazine has opened its pages to a more extensive Canadian content. Originally edited by Diane Keating and Robert Morrison (now edited by Robert Morrison, Gilbert Plaw and Elspeth Cameron), *Anthol* has functioned and continues to function as its title implies: it anthologizes current poetry. Over the course of the last five years, most of Montreal's younger poets have appeared within its pages.

More important, perhaps, than the little magazine in the development of the current Montreal poetry movement have been the establishing of a poet-run reading series at the Véhicule Art Gallery and the activities of Montreal's small presses.

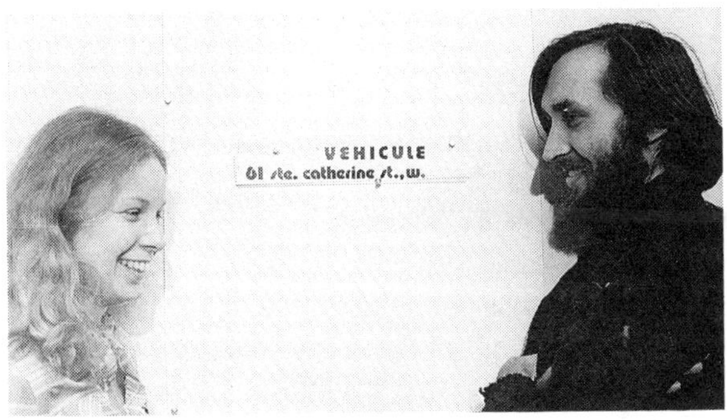

Claudia Lapp and Michael Harris. First reading at Véhicule Art Gallery, December 1972.

Another step in establishing a sense of a poetic community was taken in the fall of 1973 when Claudia Lapp and Michael Harris organized the first reading series at Véhicule, one of Montreal's parallel galleries. This provided local poets with a place to be seen and heard, the universities having opted for presenting readings by established poets from other places. In 1974, Artie Gold and Endre Farkas organized a mammoth series of thirty-seven readings at Véhicule. Virtually every local poet writing something worth hearing was given a reading. This was another important step in creating a scene and a sense of community that reached out beyond the smaller circles of writers who were known to one another. Véhicule series continues, having been run in 1975-1976 by G.C. Ian Burgess, in 1976-1977 by Robert Galvin, John McAuley and Stephen Morrissey, and this current year by Tom Konyves.

In the past in Montreal one could locate the trends and schools of poetry in the city through the little magazines that were being printed in mimeo or gestetner form. At this time, with most of the magazines adhering to an eclectic policy, it becomes easier to find the groups or schools by looking at Montreal's small presses. There are currently three major small presses operational in Montreal: Bonsecours Editions, New Delta (formerly Delta Can) and Véhicule Press (Louis Dudek's DC Press having recently ceased publication, there also remain several personal presses—Asylum, CrossCountry Press, Sunken Forum Press, Villeneuve—which have only brought out the occasional title and which function primarily as outlets for the people running them; in this they are individual rather than group minded).

Bonsecours Editions is run by G.C. Ian Burgess. The notable quality of Burgess' work as well as those he has published—Patricia Renée Ewing, Joan Thornton-McLeod, and Carole Ten Brink—is that it is predisposed towards the mythopoeic, following in the tradition of the 1950s Northrop Frye school; this work is, at times, reminiscent of the work of Jay Macpherson and Gwendolyn MacEwen. Of this group of poets Thornton-McLeod has shown herself to be the more perfect craftsperson. She is capable of going beyond the "mythic" into other realms of poetic expression, having written some strong political poems and several strikingly tender love poems.

New Delta is currently being run by the editorial board of Glen Siebrasse, Richard Sommer, and Michael Harris. New Delta's publications include books of poetry by Marc Plourde, David Solway, Peter Van Toorn, Bob McGee, Anne McLean, Richard Sommer, and Michael Harris. Each of these poets has published some distinctive verse; despite their differing poetic stances, all of them find a point of relation between their own writing and varying poetic traditions. One might also suggest that the general tendency of the New Delta poets is to consider the poem as a "well-wrought urn," following the modernists in their overriding concern with form, as opposed to the post-modern, phenomenological, composition by field predilection of the Vehicule poets. Though having turned to the writing of prose in the past few years, Marc Plourde has written some excellent poetry of description which evokes rural Quebec scenes and landscapes, as well as poems dealing with the malaise of urban living and two striking reminiscences of his grandmother. Plourde has a fine eye for detail and a gentle direct manner in his composition; without strain, his poems manage to locate what is truly "poetic" in certain situations and instances. David Solway is a poet who began writing during the Montreal movement of the sixties. Having written in various forms over the past fifteen years, Solway's recent work shows an attempt to synthesize traditional poetic forms with contemporary events and language. Like Cohen and Layton, Solway has contracted a case of pure fascination regarding Greece, so that many of his poems deal with Greek place names and themes. When his poems succeed, they display an intriguing working together of established metrical conventions with the modern idiom. Peter Van Toorn's poem "In Guildenstern Country" is the most free-wheeling, structurally innovative poem written in Montreal to date, one that succeeds as a fantastically adventuresome experiment in language, running a wild gauntlet in its use of slang and the vernacular. Van Toorn is an interesting paradox in that he seems equally at home writing in experimental and traditional forms. Recently, he has been working some interesting turns upon the form of the sonnet. Also known for a time as a sonneteer, Bob McGee has taken, in the last two years, a different turn in his writing. McGee's first book, *Three Dozen Sonnets*, was a wild and woolly collection of experimental sonnets written by a young poet of nineteen years. Now, at twenty-five, McGee has begun to write a much more tightly controlled, highly formal poetry. The free-flowing music of his earlier work has been replaced by a flatter, more deliberate tone. Anne McLean's tie with tradition manifests itself in her use of the genre of the western as a mode of poetic exploration in her first book *Lil*. Deriving her main character from Diamond Lil in Edward Dorn's *Slinger*, McLean has written a long narrative centering upon a woman who is both ahead of and out of her own time. The poetry of Richard Sommer reflects the influence of Far Eastern poetic forms, particularly that of the haiku. His recent book, *Milarepa*, extends this Eastern concern to a retelling of the life of Milarepa, focusing upon his relationships with his teacher and his own chief disciple. Sommer is as much aware of the philosophy underlying the poetic forms of the East as he is of the forms themselves. Michael Harris is a poet who is also very much aware of the traditions of poetry, having paid particular attention to English ballad forms and the contemporary verse of English poet Ted Hughes.

The Vehicule poets are those who are on the press's editorial board (Endre Farkas, Artie Gold, and myself), and those who have been published by Véhicule and maintain some affiliation with the Véhicule Poetry series. This group includes Artie Gold, Endre Farkas, myself, Claudia Lapp, Stephen Morrissey, John McAuley and Tom Konyves. This group is quite diverse in their writing styles and influences. Artie Gold would claim Frank O'Hara as one of his poetic fathers; his poetry shows an O'Hara and Spicerish influence, yet his poems are distinctly his own, reflecting a humourous and individual world view. His personal poems are not lyrics as much as metaphorical dramatizations. He is equally at home with the elegiac and pornographic; Gold is a poet who knows all the rules of poetry and when to break them. The poetry of Endre Farkas is primarily lyrical in quality, although his recent serial poem, *Murders In The Welcome Café*, is a metaphysical exploration of the detective genre and the nature of perception. Farkas also experiments with concrete and sound poetry. Claudia Lapp is a poet who works with sound in many of her poems, utilizing the principles of chant and song; she has also written some lovely erotic poems. Her recent work shows an increasing concern with women's mythic and worldly roles. Stephen Morrissey is one of Montreal's more experimental poets, having worked for some time in the realms of concrete and sound poetry. With his wife Pat Walsh he has been giving performances of sound poetry for several years. When writing in a more conventional style, Morrissey writes poems that read like extended haiku, adhering to a sharp precision of image. All of his work is marked by a constant concern with aesthetics. John McAuley is a poet who tends to work in long extended serial forms. His poem "What Henry Hudson Found" is a poetic exploration of historical realities; a recently completed work, *Mattress Testing*, concerns itself with the metaphysics of sex. Tom Konyves is another poet inclined towards the experimental wing of Montreal poetry. Having started out very much in the Montreal tradition of Jewish romantic lyricism, Konyves has, over the last two years, forsaken that in order to begin writing a kind of neo-surrealist anti-poetry which is often both humourous and powerful. The primary characteristic shared by these poets is their inclination towards the exploration of poetic techniques and varying subject matter. They can be seen to be essentially concerned with the aesthetic problems of composition and the hidden poetic qualities that are to be discovered in history, popular culture, acts of perception, and man's complex relationships with food, sleep and sex. Their poetry attempts to distill some essence out of what most would consider to be mundane reality.

There are several poets who have no direct relationship with these small presses, yet who are a part of the current scene. Laurence Hutchman's first book, *Explorations*, was published by Dudek's now defunct DC Press. Hutchman, like Marc Plourde, is most at home with a poetry of descriptive detail; his best poems are those which bear a close relation to the doctrines of Imagism. August Kleinzahler's first book, *The Sausage Master of Minsk*, is a short collection of well-crafted verse. In Fraser Sutherland's poetry one finds an alternating concern with the tragedies of life's losers and the aesthetic possibilities of art.

Although the Montreal little magazines do not proselytize in favour of new schools of poetry, they do provide a varied and lively forum for the new Montreal poetry. Though, in the main, eclectic, they have their own idiosyncrasies and personalities. *Davinci* was started in 1973 by Allan Bealy and puts out one issue a year. Bealy is a conceptual artist rather than a poet; hence, each issue of *Davinci* works as an artistic piece rather than as a run of the mill literary magazine. *Montreal Poems*, edited by Keitha MacIntosh, is now going into its fourth issue and, as the title indicates, prints Montreal poetry. The magazine is basically eclectic and publishes a broad spectrum of Montreal writing composed in various styles. *CrossCountry*, edited by Robert Galvin, Jim Mele and myself, is a magazine attempting to extend itself beyond Montreal and beyond Canada, and is working towards creating a North American poetic dialogue. *CrossCountry* No. 3/4 was a special issue devoted exclusively to Montreal poetry written in both French and English, trying to establish some awareness of poetic activities in the city's two primary cultures.

There are currently two magazines coming out of the English universities: *Process* and *Los*, originating from Sir George Williams and Loyola College respectively. Accordingly, they feature student writers although occasionally publishing local work from outside the university. At McGill there is another magazine in the making: *Atropos*, which will try to establish itself as a significant literary review.

The Alchemist is edited by Marco Fraticelli. Its poetic bias is towards poetry dealing with the possibilities of myth. Possibly Montreal's funniest little magazine, *mouse eggs* is unedited and mostly publishes the work of the Vehicule poets. It is mimeographed in lots of fifty copies and usually appears in celebration of a certain holiday with some poems written especially in honour of the event. In a little over a year *mouse eggs* has appeared thirteen times, making it Montreal's most published little mag. *Maker*, a newsletter of poetry and poetics, is edited by John McAuley and is sent out to a select mailing list. It prints concrete poetry as well as writing of a more conventional nature. The neo-Dada and neo-surrealist spirit in Montreal finds its embodiment in Tom Konyves' *Hh*. The writing therein ranges from the experimentally sublime to the ridiculous. Its first cousin, *Every Man His Own Football*, echoes the more political German Dadaist attitude. It appears as a supplement to *Hh*. Montreal's news little magazine is *Versus*, edited by Fred Louder and Robyn Sarah. Despite the magazine's fighting title, its editorial policy is most liberal. Lastly, there is the *Montreal Poets Information Exchange Newsletter*, run now for over two years by Mattie Falworth. The newsletter keeps the community up to date on readings and publications.

The current Montreal poetry movement is not one that has risen out of the ashes of the failed Montreal scene of the sixties, but rather has taken its impetus from the diversification of and experimentation in poetry that took place across Canada during that time. Poets in Montreal write in many different voices and styles; they write a significant poetry and continue to explore the possibilities of poetry. The seventies in Montreal is not a time of retreat into the conservatism that has become prevalent in all aspects of Canadian society. As poets should, the Montreal poets who write today continue to work with the modern colloquial idiom and to consider the situations of contemporary life in an attempt to uncover the poetic honey that's to be found hidden beneath the rubble of this age's lifestyle and language.

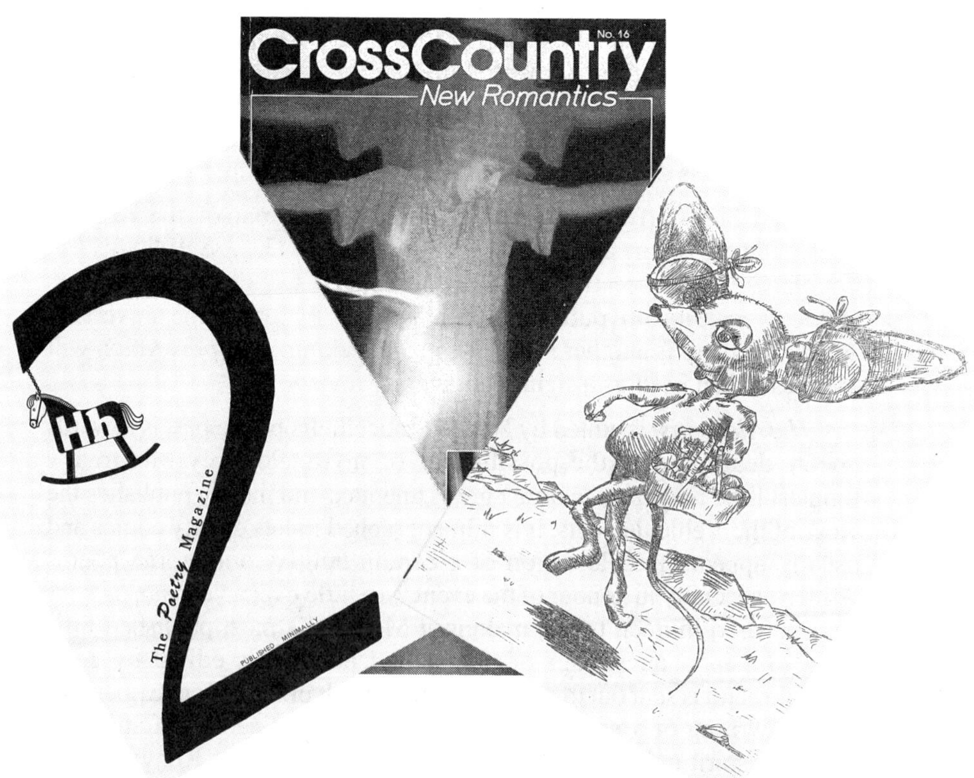

A Second Look at English Poetry in Montreal

David O'Rourke

CVII 4:4, Spring 1980

Ken Norris' article in *CVII*, "Montreal English Poetry in the Seventies," is the updated version of "Poetic Honey: The English Poetry Scene in Montreal," and a great improvement over the "Introduction" to the anthology *Montreal English Poetry of the Seventies.*[1] The revised article is less a manifesto than the "Introduction," and exhibits more judiciousness in the selection of a critical jargon than "Poetic Honey." The phenomenon of anglophone poets choosing to write in English is no longer considered a political stance, and terms such as "movement" and "tradition" are exercised with a little more wisdom and care. Norris is at his strongest when chronicling events in the last two decades of Montreal poetry. As such, "Montreal English Poetry in the Seventies" must be seen as an important catalogue of names, dates, and little magazine titles which have figured in the recent poetic history of Montreal. It is when Mr. Norris places emphasis, or engages in interpretation, that the weaknesses begin to show.

The opening paragraph contains a rather mystifying statement: "The Montreal poet also recognizes that, as a Quebecois, he is isolated from the rest of English Canada and that there is not an open line of communication running between himself and it." The sentiment is echoed later in the essay: "Because of Montreal's relative isolation from the rest of Canada, magazines in Montreal have, in the past few years, come to exist as survival outlets for Montreal writing." Norris' comments are quite appropriate for francophone writing, but do not make a great deal of sense when applied to anglophone poetry. He is not alone in this position, however, and offers an excerpt from an old issue of *Booster & Blaster* to substantiate his point:

> *The Montreal Free Poet, Booster & Blaster* publishes Montreal poets only. There is a reason in this. We are an English-speaking community, physically circumscribed within a larger French-speaking community, but paradoxically, a minority which shares a majority English-speaking consciousness. This is difficult politics and should create a poetry of meaningful content and commitment. Too much poetry in English Canada is a poetry of experiences, a recording without reflection. Here in Quebec that approach is unacceptable. Here, great English-speaking poetry will be written, not only confessional but historical, dealing with Quebec's distinctive and local reality—survival.[2]

The author of this statement, a Mr. Raymond Gordy, is not incorrect in his portrayal of the anglophone situation in Montreal; that this justifies a closed magazine, however, seems as silly as the suggestion that English Montreal poems are cut off at some border-point, physical or psychological, between Quebec and the rest of Canada. If a Montreal poet cannot get his work published outside of his own city, perhaps it is because his poetry is not that good. The only drawback for the anglophone poet based in Montreal, vis à vis publication in English Canada, is that he is not geographically close enough to become familiar with any of the editors, a regrettable but not often articulated criterion for a number of the "little mags." The parochial spirit which would have a person celebrate a closed magazine can sometimes lead to harder drugs. Poetry may become a sort of contest, garrison versus garrison. Norris' history is often infused with just such a spirit: "The sixties were an interesting time in Montreal, for it was the time that Montreal lost the poetic spotlight it had held for over thirty years to the Vancouver *Tish* poets and other manifestations of New Wave Canada."

But the most serious flaw in "Montreal English Poetry in the Seventies" is the author's predilection for movements: a preference which colours his vision and a bias which often tyrannizes his findings. The treatment of "the modernist cause" is routine, save for the exclusion of Patrick Anderson; from 1925 to the late fifties a "tradition of social realism" has taken root in Montreal, one which found its way into the poetry of the following decade. Irving Layton, Leonard Cohen, and Louis Dudek are seen as the most important influences upon the Montreal poets of the sixties. It might be remembered from Norris' "Introduction" that Layton and Cohen were considered representative of a "Jewish romantic lyricism" and a "Dionysian element," whereas Dudek stood for the "Apollonian counterpoint," "larger poetic structures" ('in which to explore Western philosophy and aesthetics') and "rationalist constructions."[3] In "Montreal English Poetry in the Seventies," Dudek is identified with social realism, and Layton/Cohen with "the poetry of Jewish tradition" and "the poetry of personality"; in addition, Cohen is associated with a "sardonic black romanticism." When all these comments are combined, it becomes evident that there is not a great deal that Messrs. Layton, Cohen, and Dudek do not represent for Mr. Norris. It is certainly safe to refer to the early poetry of both Dudek and Layton as "social realism," but by the fifties such a label becomes a misnomer for Dudek and too simplistic for Layton. Likewise, the allusion to Layton/Cohen's work as "the poetry of personality," while in part correct, misses completely the significance of the persona of "the poet"—frequently for Layton a symbol of Jesus as overman, and for Cohen an icon of Christ on the cross. It would be nice to believe that the poets of at least one generation could turn from British and American models long enough to imitate Canadian masters, and it does not seem that surprising that the country's first authentic poetic tradition would be based in Montreal. Unfortunately, Norris has not rigorously marked what could be one of the most important paths in Canadian poetry. On the contrary, he dismisses the Montreal poetry scene of the sixties because of its apparent "conservative" spirit. He seems more interested in schools of thought than significant work, more at home in charting movements than accurately tracing development.

The kind of conservatism Norris objects to centers upon the question of technique: Montreal's "failure" in the sixties is seen primarily as a consequence of its having "nothing new to offer in terms of poetics and poetic techniques"; the scene is doomed because its poets ignore "an influx of various new ideas and experiments in poetry, ranging from Black Mountain to Dada to North American Indian rituals." In short, "Poets writing in the west simply had more to offer." Norris' "spotlight" assessment might well be correct, but it ignores the fact that poets such as Layton, Cohen, Dudek, and Scott were still producing in Montreal. It might be pointed out that an important characteristic of the city's poetry has always been the outspokenness of its leading figures: Smith's manifestos in the twenties, Sutherland's salvos in the forties, and Irving Layton's finger ever since. Montreal poets have shown a willingness to experiment—witness the influence of Louis Dudek alone—but rarely, it is important to note, at the expense of content. It is possible that Norris does not draw this artificial line, but his emphasis upon technique is unsettling, particularly in view of the city's history of dialectical concerns: social, philosophical, native, cosmopolitan, interpersonal and psychological. The problem of Montreal's having "nothing new to offer in terms of poetics and poetic techniques" is rated as being more significant than the possibility that its younger poets actually had nothing new to say. It is in this that they may be perceived as being "pale imitations" of Dudek, Layton and Cohen, not in the sense that they were given to traditional forms.

The picture brightens for Mr. Norris toward the end of the sixties with the arrival of George Bowering in Montreal. In Norris' "Introduction" it is claimed that Bowering's "most important contribution to the new generation of Montreal poets was the institution of a series of readings at Sir George which exposed them to the diverse experimentation that was taking place across Canada and the U.S."[4] Norris might be quite right in underlining the impact of Sir George on Montreal poetry. The sixties saw the concrete campus more responsive than either McGill or Loyola to contemporary North American trends. Getting on the American reading tour, Sir George brought in Creeley, Snyder, Duncan, Berrigan, and a number of other innovative poets while the more traditional universities leaned toward the more establishment writers. In "Montreal English Poetry in the Seventies," however, it is clarified that it was not George Bowering, but rather a faculty committee which instituted these same readings. Even so, Bowering is seen as an important influence, having "awakened" creative writing students such as John McAuley, Tom Konyves and Artie Gold to "the new possibilities of poetry."

It was not until the Fall of 1973 that the reading series at the Véhicule Art Gallery got off the ground: that is, two years after Bowering had left Montreal. Its originators were Claudia Lapp and Michael Harris. Michael Harris, it might be noted, is not known for a commitment to Black Mountain, Dada, or Indian ritual; nevertheless, "This was an important step in creating a scene and a sense of community that reached out beyond the smaller circles of writers who were known to each other." Norris also updates: the Véhicule poetry series was run in 1974 by Artie Gold and Endre Farkas; in 1975-76 by G.C. Burgess; the following year by Robert Galvin, John McAuley and Stephen Morrissey; and in 1977-78 by Tom Konyves. The names begin to sound familiar as Norris draws his hyphenated line. In the meantime, Harris has made the trek to New Delta.

Véhicule Poetry Series '76

Oct. 31	JON SILKIN
Nov. 14	OPAL L. NATIONS
Nov. 28	STEVE McCAFFERY
Dec. 5	KEITHA K. MacINTOSH
Dec. 12	MATTIE FALWORTH & GUY BIRCHARD
Dec. 19	OPEN READING

ALL READINGS SUNDAY AT 2:00 pm

Véhicule Art, 61 St. Catherine Street W., Montreal, Quebec

(514) 844-9623

Norris' history is concluded with a discussion of three of Montreal's current anglophone presses. Bonsecours Editions is viewed as "predisposed towards the mythopoeic," and its poets are praised for the quality of their work. Compared to the next two presses, however, Bonsecours Editions is rather neutral.

New Delta is seen as Glen Siebrasse, Richard Sommer and Michael Harris (editorial board), as well as Marc Plourde, David Solway, Peter

Van Toorn, Bob McGee, and Anne McLean. According to Norris, "Each of these poets has published some distinctive verse; despite their different poetic stances, all of them find a point of relation between their writing and varying poetic traditions." This then is the traditional group, the bulk of whom have been around since the sixties. Three (David Solway, Peter Van Toorn and Marc Plourde) have appeared in Ralph Gustafson's *Penguin Book of Canadian Verse;*[5] more recently, Michael Harris has found acceptance in *The Atlantic Monthly*.[6] Both Plourde and Van Toorn are highly regarded by Mr. Norris, though Van Toorn's facility with both experimental and traditional forms is viewed, for some reason, as an "interesting paradox." Sommer and McLean get mild approval for explorations of the East and Diamond Lil respectively, but Solway, McGee, and Harris—perhaps the best of the active New Delta poets—do not fare so well. Norris remarks of Solway that "many of his poems deal with Greek place names and themes," and that, "When his poems succeed they display an intriguing working together of established metrical conventions with the modern idiom." McGee's first book is praised but Norris notes, "The freeflowing music of his earlier work has been replaced by a flatter, more deliberate tone." Of Harris, all that is said is "Michael Harris is a poet who is also very much aware of the traditions of poetry, having paid particular attention to English ballad forms and the contemporary verse of English poet Ted Hughes."

The Vehicule poets are listed as Artie Gold, Endre Farkas, Mr. Norris himself (editorial board), and Claudia Lapp, Stephen Morrissey, John McAuley and Tom Konyves. Gold "is a poet who knows all the rules of poetry and when to break them." Farkas "experiments with concrete and sound poetry." John McAuley "tends to work in long extended serial forms"; he also edits *Maker*, which prints "concrete poetry as well as writing of a more conventional nature." Mr. McAuley is quoted in the *MPIE Newsletter* as stating, "I am interested in: concrete poetry, manifestoes, experimental linear poetry, fluxus, dada-post-dada, intermedia, marginals, etc."[7] Finally, Tom Konyves has forsaken "the Montreal tradition of Jewish romantic lyricism" for "a kind of neo-surrealist anti-poetry which is often both humourous and powerful." According to Mr. Norris, and one would include his own experimental work, "The primary characteristic shared by these poets is their inclination towards the exploration of poetic techniques and varying subject matter." That might be an understatement, but it is unfortunate that Norris does not go further to determine whether or not all this experimentation has produced any poetry of value.

"Montreal English Poetry in the Seventies" ends with the following observation: "The current Montreal poetry movement is not one that has risen out of the ashes of the failed Montreal scene of the sixties, but rather has taken its impetus from the diversification of and experimentation in poetry that took place across Canada during that time." In the light of his commentary upon Montreal's little presses, Norris' summation is particularly concerned with only one group of poets: influenced by George Bowering and the Sir George Williams readings, it is Mr. Norris' own group, Vehicule, which is in the vanguard of experimentation in Montreal. Fellow Vehicule poet, Artie Gold, not surprisingly concurs in a recent article in *Books in Canada*: "Meanwhile, Véhicule Press seems to be pulling ahead, somehow ending up with more interesting poets (perhaps only my bias, but expect it)."[8] "Perhaps only my bias, but expect it": a curious interpolation. In contrast to Véhicule, New Delta exhibits a conservative point of view, apparently clinging "too rigidly to the poetic values of the past."

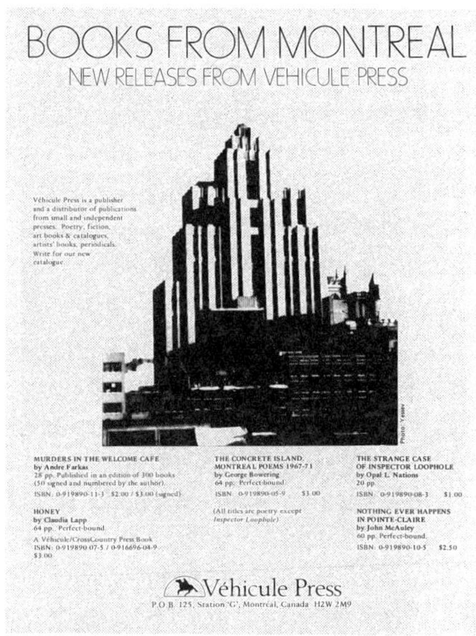

One way of understanding a battle is to simply look at who is on whose side. In his critical work on Montreal poetry, Ken Norris draws a rather graphic line right down the centre. He is quite honest about which side he is on, and just as confident about which side is going to win. Montreal may have lost the round of the sixties to *Tish* and New Wave Canada, but Véhicule is already making gains in this decade. Of course the problem with such a competitive approach to poetry is that one always needs an opponent. Enter New Delta.

It is difficult to watch these contemporary developments in Montreal poetry without going back to the *First Statement/Preview* battle royal of the early forties. Ken Norris comes on like a John Sutherland and Véhicule's voice, though local, has an American accent. In contrast, New Delta stands for cosmopolitan and polished verse. It seems a case of déjà vu: Véhicule has the printing press and New Delta has the poets. The case is not that simple, however. Norris lacks John Sutherland's critical vision. Véhicule's local concerns appear cliquish, and the interest in Black Mountain/*Tish* is a decade or so late. Ultimately, of course, a school must rest upon the best work of its students, and this may prove to be the biggest hurdle of all for the Vehicule poets. There is certainly nothing wrong with technical exploration and, in spite of the nationalist influence in Canadian letters, there is nothing immoral about admitting to an

American influence. Unfortunately, for all their experimentation, it is not that obvious that the Vehicule poets have made any important discoveries; rather, one senses an "echoing" of David McFadden and "pale imitations" of Black Mountain and *Tish*. Even more regrettable is the fact that the Vehicule poets have sacrificed content in order to be "avant-garde." While John McAuley's *A Monograph Illustrating the Chocolate Laws of Milkie O'Henry* is only the most obvious example, the tendency toward superficiality may be perceived in most of the Vehicule poets.[9] Capable of both the exceptional "O'Hara Elegy" and "Down Below" in 1973, Artie Gold has been reduced to writing of his cats:

> I confess
> I cannot
> put broken cats
> back together but neither
> can god).
>
> in his effort
> to be free
> or seem so
> our big grey
> ran miles away[10]

Likewise, with "The Gypsy Judge Answers" and "Mao Tse Tung as Hero" to his credit, Endre Farkas risks being taken seriously as a poet with the whimsical *Murders in the Welcome Café*. Even then, as though despite the author's will to be clever, the poems making up Chapters Seven and Nine succeed, as does part of Chapter Thirteen:

> ...there are summer nights
> when you come close to yourself
> so close
> you split and experience the lag
> and to know something real
> you must first learn to kill it[11]

Ken Norris is not always so fortunate with his creative work. While it is a good sign that he has been able to leave behind the artificiality of *Vegetables* (1975; rpt. Montreal: Véhicule, 1976), he does not successfully integrate his own experience with that of the world "writing" him in *Report on the Second Half of the Twentieth Century* (Montreal: CrossCountry, 1977), nor is he able to invoke the vision and claustrophobic sensibility apparent in his excellent "Houdini." *Proverbsi* (Montreal: Asylum, 1977), written with Tom Konyves has nothing at all to do with poetry—consisting entirely of one-liners meant for the most part to be funny ("No man can serve two masters but can easily service two mistresses"). The same juvenilia permeates Konyves' most recent book, *No Parking* ("My feet don't stink anymore/since you've sent me that heavenly foot powder"). When Konyves is able to resist a joke—which is rare—something like "On the Suicidal Death of Pierre Paradis: Oct. 6, 1975" surfaces:

On the first cut
of the album, right
at the beginning
it's that horn.[12]

John McAuley displays a similar editorial carelessness with the revised version of *nothing ever happens in pointe-claire* (Montreal: Véhicule, 1977) including within its pages a number of little magazine rejection letters. It is not clear what interest these letters are thought to hold for the reader, and it is not surprising that "fallout flash" may be the only poem worthy of attention in the book. Claudia Lapp's *Honey* (1973; rpt. Montreal: Véhicule/CrossCountry, 1977) is marked in its sincerity and frankness of expression, but it is unfortunate that the poet is not able to shake more often the concern articulated at the beginning of the book: "don't leave the bed too soon—/you can't come with words"; still, the poem "Shoes" works and the directness is occasionally refreshing. The only Vehicule poet to thus far happily marry experiment with quality, however, is Stephen Morrissey. "Poem" ('there are seashells and cats'), "New Year's Day 4 a.m." and "regard as sacred," are examples of a mind interested in the nature of perception, both as it affects the art of poetry and as it reveals the world outside of books. Morrissey attaches a great deal of care to his work, suppressing the trivial for the universal and the rhetorical for the poetic.

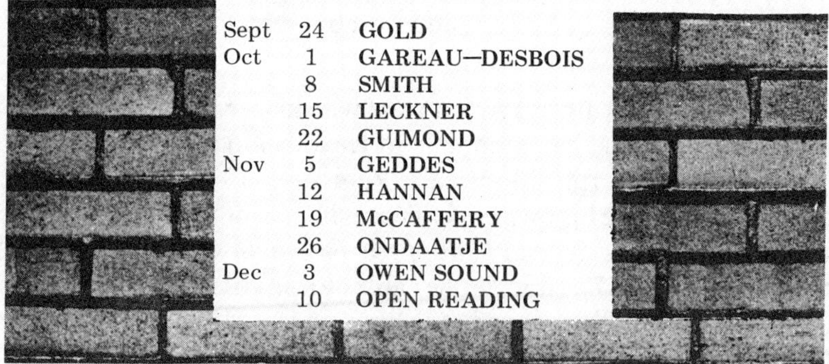

In a letter to the *Montreal Star* dated January 7, 1978, Carol H. Leckner states:

> The Montreal poetry scene is by no means a closed one. But it is dominated by Farkas, Norris, Konyves et al, because they are willing to do the work. There is nothing stopping anyone else from editing, publishing and running poetry series.[13]

Ms. Leckner's point is not without merit, but the fact of the matter is that most poets would rather write than edit, run a printing press, or set up a poetry series. It becomes the responsibility of those people who do to strive for some kind of objectivity, at least in reporting events to the rest of the country.

Interested in new movements, Ken Norris may have overestimated the importance of Véhicule in his critical work. A number of passing references to New Delta, however, suggest the possibility of a genuine literary tradition in Montreal. At one point in his articles, Norris groups Klein, Layton and Cohen; at another point: Layton, Cohen and Solway. If Norris is correct in his contention of a "Jewish tradition" reaching into the sixties, and if indeed it is possible to shake of "the ashes" and rise from the dead, then the figure of David Solway should loom significantly in any serious study of Montreal poetry. His attraction to mythology, Biblical and Greek, his view of the poet as slightly overman and slightly underdog, and his conception of his situation, psychological and post-modern, as something akin to a furnace, all tie Solway in with Klein, Layton and Cohen. But to depart from the theory of a strictly "Jewish tradition," one more name might be added: that of Michael Harris. The theme of grace and "how to get it" is not one that is new to Montreal. For Layton, "grace" is human divinity with a Jewish-Nietzschean twist; for Cohen, it is a kind of sainthood made accessible by a curious sort of martyrdom; for Harris, it is a stasis, a momentary stay from disintegration and chaos—how it is gained is often less important than how it can be maintained.

If there is such as thing as a Canadian literary tradition, Montreal may be the first place to look. Neither Solway nor Harris are derivative of their major predecessors; quite the opposite, like Klein, Layton and Cohen, their interests seem to lie more with world literature than in anything that has come out of Canada. But a tradition does not have to mean a succession of imitative poets, be they experimental or conservative. Rather, it might consist of a number of generations linked by certain thematic concerns: often through the very process of rebellion. For Solway and Harris, and perhaps Mr. McGee, there has been much in the way of obstacles: Layton, force of personality; Cohen, the sense of elect; and even Dudek, make it new. Moreover, the giants are still alive and kicking despite their exclusion from Norris' anthology. Perhaps one should wait for the dust to settle after all—in the meanwhile, fireworks are lighting up the streets of Montreal.

—David O'Rourke
York University

Notes

[1] Ken Norris, "Montreal English Poetry in the Seventies." *CVII*, Vol. 3, No. 3 (January 1978), pp. 8-13; Ken Norris, "Poetic Honey: The English Poetry Scene in Montreal," *Essays on Canadian Writing*, No. 6 (Spring 1977), pp. 66-76; Ken Norris and Andre Farkas, eds., *Montreal English Poetry of the Seventies* (Montreal: Véhicule, 1977).

[2] "Montreal English Poetry in the Seventies," p. 9.

[3] "Introduction," *Montreal English Poetry of the Seventies*, p. x.

[4] *Ibid.*, p. xi.

[5] Ralph Gustafson, ed., *The Penguin Book of Canadian Verse*, rev. ed. (1958; rpt. London: Cox & Wyman, 1975).

[6] Michael Harris, "The Gamekeeper," *The Atlantic Monthly*, Vol 242, No. 6 (December 1978), p. 81; Michael Harris, "The Ice Castle," *The Atlantic Monthly*, Vol. 243, No. 3 (March 1979), p. 122.

[7] Ari Snyder, "Sparrow, Owls, Loons," *Montreal Poets' Information Exchange Newsletter*, Vol. 2, No. 10 (July 1977), p. 5.

[8] Artie Gold, "Poetic Mêlée Drama," *Books in Canada*, Vol. 8, No. 2 (February 1979), p. 12.

[9] John McAuley, *A Monograph Illustrating the Chocolate Laws by Milkie O'Henry* (Montreal: Hy Jack, 1973); reprinted in *nothing ever happens in pointe-claire* (Montreal: Véhicule, 1977).

[10] Artie Gold, *Some of the Cat Poems* (Montreal: CrossCountry, 1978), p. 2.

[11] Andre Farkas, *Murders in the Welcome Café* (Montreal: Véhicule, 1977), Chapter 13.

[12] Tom Konyves, *No Parking* (Montreal: Véhicule, 1978), p. 38.

[13] Carol H. Leckner, "Montreal Waiting for Poets," *The Montreal Star*, 7 January 1978. Ms. Leckner is a Montreal poet.

PROVERBSI #45

The inside is greater than the outside.

An Open Letter to David O'Rourke Concerning Montreal Poetry

Ken Norris

CVII 5:1, Autumn 1980

Dear David,

I read your "A Second Look at English Poetry in Montreal" with interest and amusement; interest because it's flattering to be so extensively paraphrased, even if then after you proceed to disagree with me, amusement because your article is so out of date. I suppose that if you had taken the trouble to revise it each time it came bouncing back from the magazines that passed on it, the article would have done more service to its subject. The Montreal scene that you're looking at doesn't exist any more; it's gone through a myriad of changes.

A few comments seem to be in order. First, I find it a bit strange that you attempt to extract an aesthetic manifesto out of what I've written in what have been, essentially, descriptive articles. I suppose that, in attempting to be objective, a bias has undoubtedly slipped in here and there, but I don't feel that my articles have been very polemical. Not that I don't have strong views of what's been happening in poetry here, but I've tried to temper them in the past when relating "the facts" about Montreal poetry in the seventies. But I'm not adverse to laying my position out, and I suppose I'll do that in a few paragraphs' time.

Beyond not being able to understand why Endre Farkas isn't given any credit for co-authoring the "Introduction" to *Montreal English Poetry of the Seventies* and why we are reprimanded for leaving Cohen, Layton, and Dudek out of an anthology which is obviously a collection of younger poets, a new generation as it were, I find it strange that you can't really comprehend the regionalization of poetry that's been going on in this country in the 1970s, and which has been very strong in Quebec. After the great Centennial centralizing efforts of the late sixties, we've witnessed, in the seventies, the sprouting up of countless regional presses all across the country. I think this has been in response to Ontario's rather bizarre concept of what Canada is. Writers in other parts of the country seem to be faced with the alternatives of changing their aesthetics and going to Toronto to "make it," or else concentrating their energies on local community activity. After the 1960s burn-out here, when some poets went crazy trying to become Irving Layton and others got discouraged when, after learning to play the guitar, they discovered they couldn't be the next Leonard Cohen, writers (or at least some of them) got sensible; they started building from the ground up again, just as Layton and Dudek had done with Sutherland in the forties, and with Souster doing Contact Press out of Toronto in the 1950s. Your inability to understand why locally based little magazines have sprung up here and elsewhere betrays a lack of understanding as to what the little magazine is and what function it serves. Your statement that "If a Montreal poet cannot get his work published outside of his own city, perhaps it is because his poetry is not that good" is one of the dumbest sentences I've seen in a while. Many Montreal poets *do* publish in magazines all across this country and in the United States. That, however, still does not discount the necessity for regional magazines that serve as community rallying points. To paraphrase Pound, civilization is not a one man job, nor can the creation of literature ever really be a national pursuit. Nation is a neat form of categorization, but ultimately literature is valuable within regional and international contexts.

As organizer and anthologist I suppose that if there's one thing that gets my hackles up it's the accusation of being cliquish, and I suppose that after co-editing an anthology of twenty-two Montreal poets, writing an article or two about the parameters of the scene, and after co-editing another anthology of fifty Quebec poets, I find it somewhat offensive when you reprimand me for not fulfilling the responsibilities of objectivity. I guess I also remember when Harris was working on the Quebec *CVII* issue before I became involved with it and he had arranged for about twelve poets (as I remember it, eight of what Michael termed "elder statesmen," himself and three friends) to be the poets from Quebec, whereupon I had to pry the issue open with a crow-bar to get in some other poets and to get some recognition going in the issue that Montreal does, in fact, have poets here writing in French. I feel like I live in a large community which accommodates many writers. Michael Harris, if he believes what he has said in conversation, believes that there are but three "poets" in all of Montreal.

Which leads us, I suppose, to the "New Delta/Véhicule" antagonism. I think that you're superficially right in seeing it as a continuation of the *First Statement/Preview* feud of the forties. The New Delta boys are obviously interested in British poets like Ted Hughes, New England poets like Richard Wilbur, and dead poets like Matthew Arnold. The Véhicule crowd is more Canadian and American influenced. The Delta crowd is elitist and conservative and their sense of form is retrograde and restrictive. Personally I find Solway and Harris somewhat necrophilic in their artistic tendencies; they belong to the cult of dead forms and dead animals. One personal fact worth interjecting is that Harris is a butterfly collector. This is something I find totally repulsive and perhaps reflects our varying sense of aesthetics. I like my butterflies alive and flying, not dead and preserved. The Véhicule crowd, as Louis Dudek once pointed out, is always ready to sacrifice a little immortality for a resurrection in the here and now.

I believe that we're poets committed to life first, and then art. Some may see that as a betrayal of art, but if art is dead butterflies, I think we had better start betraying it fast. Solway and Harris have followed Layton in seeing the world in terms of sex and death for so long that I don't think they're now able to distinguish between the two. If art isn't going to be a lively experience then why bother with it? I'm sorry if you find some of the Véhicule work trivial or superficial, but I can only suggest that you get a new pair of glasses and get your head screwed on straight. David Solway's view of life: "Everything is happening behind you" ("Lines Written in Dejection"); David Solway's view of poetry: "Poetry begins in innocence, yet/it ends in perpetual regret" ("Shakespeare"); Michael Harris on the nature of things: "Life, Death: small things" ("Bluebottle"). To which we say "No thanks." The Vehicule poets, by no means, believe in the sacrosanct nature (or even the melancholic value) of the past, don't intend to regret their poetry, and don't view Life and Death as small things. Everything is happening in the present, poetry is not meant as a place to deposit your bitternesses and tattered desires, it's a place to celebrate. Life and Death are very great things. Life is to be celebrated in all of its glory and its stupidity, its profundity and its ordinariness. As long as people keep conceptualizing art as the perfection of life and life as the crude materials out of which art can be made, they're going to go on feeling regret and pain. As long as poets keep writing their poems with an eye on posterity and their good reputation they're going to go on being purveyors of death, creating art that functions in the service of death, not life.

One last thing I'd like to comment upon is the "accusation" or statement that the Vehicule poets have been heavily influenced by Black Mountain and *Tish.* That's bullshit. I feel a lot more influenced by F.R. Scott and Louis Dudek than by Charles Olson, Robert Duncan, or George Bowering. Artie Gold loves Frank O'Hara and three thousand other poets. Canadian critics have gotten real sloppy, equating radical Modernism with Black Mountain, equating all American poets with Black Mountain. I've spent the last five years studying Canadian poetry and that's what I know best, and I'd say the same would be true of Farkas and Morrissey. Since John McAuley was going to do a Ph.D. dissertation on Black Mountain I would assume he knows quite a bit about Olson & crew, but then John knows a lot about Virgil and Tibullus. Konyves doesn't know Black Mountain from Black Holes, but you'd be able to better understand his work if you knew anything about European Modernism.

Personally I'm interested in developments that further the art of poetry and operate in the service of life. Spending a lot of time mulling over the anthologies of the past trying to figure out how to weasel your way into the tradition isn't my idea of what the poet or poetry is all about. I don't believe that the way of poetry is the way of capitalism. The poet has a social responsibility, and that is to aid in mankind's realization. The poet was never meant to create art objects that become "literature." To quote Layton from some years back, "Literature is the revenge society takes on the poet, its muted polite hosanna over the fact that it has blunted his shafts and rendered them harmless." The Vehicule poets have no intention of blunting their own shafts so that the reader can play the part of the happy consumer and have a gay old time, or so that you, as critic, can have that secure feeling of being happily ensconced in the hallowed halls of Art. If the artist doesn't challenge a society's set of assumptions, then who is going to?

Best,
Ken Norris

Introduction to *The Vehicule Poets*

Artie Gold

Maker Press, 1979

I would not like to see perpetrated in the calling of this collection *The Vehicule Poets* any mythic understanding that bonds exist between these poets greater than common sympathy arising from the shared perplexities of the Montreal English lifestyle.

I don't somehow feel people will understand the spirit in which seven of us have just upped and borrowed a tag none of us really wants to wear to the bitter end.

So here we are and if we are together and need a name and can't rule one house with seven different signs, well, hell, let it be *Vehicule*.

I felt it all had to be somehow qualified. I was humoured, allowed this self-conscious soliloquy.

That this collection of essential people (then) is a set or subset that would seem to exhaust with the seven is probably a claim that I should confess, like the title, is a trifle more convenient than true...nevertheless, in these seven writers and their works, *a world* begins to emerge that might merit a separate look.

Not as one, then, do we present ourselves, but AT ONCE.

So I am writing this intro somewhat in the spirit of clarification

To set aside the already disturbing conviction that people I have talked to seem to hold

A name like *The Vehicule Poets* suggests to me a principle operating to, on one hand, enumerate, on the other, exhaust. Told such a collection was desirable I nodded; all collections seem desirable, especially those of poetry.

It is hoped it will be understood that the purpose of putting seven poets into this one collection was not towards some eventual reduction to thesis

It is only to approach the individual that groups should be braved at all

(see) group here (only as an) expedient to presentation

readers in an attempt to either reinforce the number seven or to show perhaps its absurdity and erode through physical, logical process, that number back to one, will end up with definite conclusions as to why what we are doing by going at it in sevens is either, more logical than we had realized (poor stupid us) or stupider than they could have believed possible (poor doomed to fail illogical us in any case. .) .

This collection, more than an anthology, IS *a* collection, and should perhaps best be seen as a point of convergence for our convenience in the getting of our material, the poems, to readership. No great parity, stylistically cumulative or reductively minimal exists as a high or low denominator in the work of our seven.

Valentine's Day 79, Montreal

Left to right: Artie Gold, Ken Norris, Endre Farkas. Launching of *Montreal English Poetry of the Seventies.* Fall 1977.

Romantic at Heart

Endre Farkas

Romantic at heart
I flesh out my thoughts
until they are you

Too much make-up on these New York women
by now this *too much* is their skin
                                                            and anyway

with all these pamphlets
darting from palm to palm
                                                offering you everything for $10
who looks beyond

Of course these touchings
on the all asleep bus home
affects only the dreamers

                                                I am nowhere at the moment
I don't know the distance to your arms
am sensitive only to the misshape of my spine

                                                            Desires are twisted
in those mangled wires
There is no current of fidelity

I could say "I love you" to any stranger
(even you) & mean it as much as any other time

And it's really time
being out of it that locates this bus

The darkness we're shooting into/out of
permits me to float free
                                        almost melancholy
almost as anything
                                almost crying

I settle for the thought of crying

Beginnings

Endre Farkas

You move out of the score.
The first step is always into the bottomless falling dream

The colour of fear grabs you

you wake!
First light is a surprise

call it morning.

You are brave now
you have no choice

Start again from here
where the alphabet of form don't censor us.

From here an old barn door opens in triple image

Forgotten
the time when the bellyache was the sweet pain of the
                                        becoming of a god
        (as common a desire
        as now is the ordering out for a midnight meal
        and the chances of being it
                                                open later than that
For birth
From wombs constantly waking
becoming blood familiar with the route

Soft eyes soft focus relieve the tired

For now
Each morning is sipped from a favourite cup
and not a single impossible argument is burnt.

What is left is us
                    (on the ledge, unpacking our halos
hold them to the light
spit through them
watch comets laugh their way into the heavens

Untitled

Artie Gold

I have been thinking a great deal
about my bike that will be stolen.

I don't like things whose inevitability
works against me.

Why have you driven through my heart?
Make that   what.

Untitled

Artie Gold

                                        life.

                                        in a sense
it is the exact opposite of what we want   and
that opposite isn't death
                                but fence.
somewhere   over   the rainbow
you see, it's parabolic.
sometimes stretched out on drugs that make me taller
I sway over two kingdoms of sidewalk concrete   adjacent
but over the line.   clothes vanish through the magic agency
                                                                of drugs
naked to my brain my genitals hang like a child's drawing
                                                                of scissors
open large enough only for the beam of life to shine through
I trap the living photon and aim it down.   my friends say: Artie,
   You have dropped your handkerchief.

Sept 14/77

qu'ode

Artie Gold

I am aware of my intolerances as do my perfections
blow off into the night/ I only ask you/ to consider me kindly
as change is full of worlds, somewhere there I am loved
even by you
memory disinherits bitterness, a distant memory
disinherits impatience   even striving towards that act.
that something you have to love to anchor yourself into the world
let be *me*.
when you say the *body* of a rabbit you turn it sideways
do me some such kindness. a forced passion perhaps. I
will reiterate (at times love is only mechanical
even stolen from the physical act.

garlic in the coffee doesn't work—why should it
but, it works better than shaving with a pistol
and why is *that* ?
it must be that the statement is one of those of
the kind/ if everybody read Poetry there'd be no war—
(of course there'd be no Prose *either*.
which doesn't work in only one of a million ways something might
(not.).
it has been a year of opposite effects
we used to buy things we couldn't afford
and bring them home in a taxi
now the rifle sights of the new budget
have brought all this to a standstill,
like one caress will, a cat.
We find ourselves on an unsure hill
all our strength & better natures
niggling, before its uninvestigated slope.
The blues is not in fossil preservation I decide.

Sept 13-14/78

Myth

Artie Gold

I mean we'd be fucking and suddenly you'd
wince: pain, we'd be miles apart—where,
would that leave me. Say I'd be gently
raking the long of your back the back of a
fingernail, just so slightly, would snag
tear down your flesh. shudder. you'd jump
dear you would hit the ceiling. Flare up
like phosphorous out of control in water
a different goddess you out of control in air.

you

Artie Gold

leaning, like a Hardy Boy
I touch my fingers lightly
to the invisible panel

if I listen, *fear* falls away
how are you ? over, the green hills
the panel swings, revealing—

revealing summer. daylight
roars from the spot. Above me
you stand like an easel

I lean my face sideways
tenderly towards you, nuzzle.
like an artist who has lost his brush

and what he'd begun to do
bending over, *was simply to retrieve it*
and then, *he fell in love with an idea...*

No Parking

Tom Konyves

To die   my hair   and live again. I am
in the middle of things, yet beginning
over and over
                                and over and over. To die
in the middle of things, yet beginning,
over mountains and skyscrapers in the middle
of things, letters, bras, disbursement of money
also that which is paid out, a viking on the waters,
spirit yet beginning, winning, foot by foot,
over and over, in the middle of things, churches,
nightmares, maidenheads, stockings on the dryer,
a kiss from the wall planted squarely on my lips
burning at the stake with onions, to die.

To die, my hair tied to stakes like Gulliver,
stretching from one end of the earth to
the other, my body floating, the sails of the earth.
Ahoy! Ahoy! To die my hair or not to
live again, in the middle of things, the apple-core
of living again, not living again, over and over
hurdles of living again or not living again, yet
beginning

To die   my hair   and live again. I am
in the middle, between north and south.
North/Alan 3455 Stanley St. 849-8294.
South/Astley 129 Anselme-Lavigne Dollard
des Ormeaux 684-2890 yet beginning, trimming
my hair, just a little off the top please,
leave the ears, I like pony tails, the
silence of airplanes, beached whales. Over
and over, in and out, first slowly, go shallow
then deep, shallow then deep, soft...soft...hard!
round, round, red light! slowly...slowly...yeah,
that's it.

To die my hair is growing long, too
long, too too long, hold it right there, don't
move, just like that, that's it, that's it, that's it.

To die my hair long, red, white streaks,
too too long, too long, too.

To die in a forest fire, in city hall, in the
evening, quietly, alone, with friends, family clothes,
rags to riches, in a car, in a plane,
in a bird, in a Superman costume, in the middle of the night,
on roller skates, red pavement, begging change,
in a hearse, in an alley, in a soft bed
not of my making, raking leaves in autumn,
smiling at the camera, hold it, just like that,
that's it, hold it, freeze!
Freezing, your arms around me, hugging me,
suffocating, strangled with my own belt,
shot! once, twice, in the head, between the eyes,
right between the eyes, the son of a bitch
shoot him right in the eyes, in the back, shot
in the back, just like that, walking down the street,
minding my own business, when, shot!
in the bathtub, in the hallway, leaning on the glass,
nose pressed to the glass, candy, in a hospital, with
nurses smiling, cleaning the bedpans,
of old age, yesterday, suddenly, in my sleep, gone.
In the middle of things, bills unpaid, laundry, coffee,
writing a letter to my congressman, in love,
determined to change watching the river flow
ho ho ho get this, throat slit,
stabbed, over and over and over, watching TV,
just relaxing, watching TV. Poisoned! For what?
I put words in your mouth.
                                        To die, in New York,
in Little Rock, in Venezuela, in a canary,
in Kingston, in New York, in California, in Chicago,
in a garage, in India with my guru, in your mouth,
in your cunt, in your ass, in your belly, in your bed,
in your garage, in you living room,
relaxing, watching Mary Hartman, Mary. In Greenwich,
at midnight, in Detroit, in New Orleans, in French,
in Spanish, in Quebec, defending the English
in Toronto, defending poetry,
in Noranda, in Alaska, in debt, in corpus delecti, inverted,
hung, well hung, in a hotel room, in Atlantic City,
under the boardwalk, insensitive, in fact,

run over and over and over, on a highway not far
from here, in a disco, in a disco-bar, in a movie theater,
smoking dope, shooting horse, Hh, never mind, let things lie,
in the middle of things, yet just beginning, 1901, 1961, 1971,
in a computer riot, in a performance just like this, hold it,
hold it! just like that! That's it!

To die, in Montreal, in Véhicule, on Sunday at 2,
in a McCaffery reading, in a review of my book,
in reply to your letter dated, antedated,
in society, in anti-society, in my underwear,
in a year, inveterate, in confession, in a bathroom
at a party, in art only, in fiction, in a water tank trick,
in diving from a plane, in climbing the impossible mountain
with Julie Andrews, in squinting at the sun,
in a playground, under a see-saw, in my lover's arms,
in my enemy's fort, scalped, dragged away and ravaged
by lions, in the mouth of the Euphrates, in the Nile,
in the Red Sea, in the St. Lawrence,
Superior, eerie. In the inn, having a couple, having
a meal, having multiple sclerosis, having my hair cut.
In a memo to mama, in your station wagon, after the dance,
in a cocktail, in the Star, and the Gazette, in the Voice,
in the Times, in the chronicle of our times, in the pride
of my youth, under my skin, in my skiwear, in my bathing
suit, Voodoo! Voodoo!

To die my hair and live again. I am in the middle
of things, yet beginning over and over and over and
over an argument, over a woman, over money, over a
cause, over a right and a wrong, over a game, yet
beginning, learning to say Da Da, moo moo cow, un-
learning horror, Mary. To die my hair and live,
with breasts like pomegranates, a tight ass, a big cock,
a sweet pussy, a lovely face,
over and over, in the morning, in the afternoon,
in the front seat, in the back seat, incognito.
To live again in the middle of things, pastures, a farm,
a penthouse with skylight streaming with the sparkling
stars, overlooking New York, overlooking everything
that has happened between us, yet beginning, a germ
of the universe, a giant among men, distinguished by
a scar on the forehead, a mole above the lip. To live

again, over and over, my soul, wearing jeans and T-shirt,
to attach myself to the infinite typewriter ribbon.

Heaven over and over must be missing an angel, over and
over and over, missing one angel, child, over and over
and over and over, cause you're here with me right now,
sweet little angel, over and over, right now, heaven,
over, your kiss, over, you came COD, over, I'm captured,
over, it's so good, so good, so good, over, filled with
tenderness, over and over.

Yet beginning, in the
middle of things, which is the fire that emanated from
the celestial fire, when that firmament is illumined
there become revealed four mystical groupings of letters,
each beginning in the middle of things, Mary.
In the middle of things revealed, ships, customs
houses, elm trees, dakini, *hostie*, Houdini, in-
spector, window-maker, pasta-maker, cloud-maker,
in the middle yet beginning over and over, to die
and live again, just like that, hold it, freeze!
That's it? That's it.

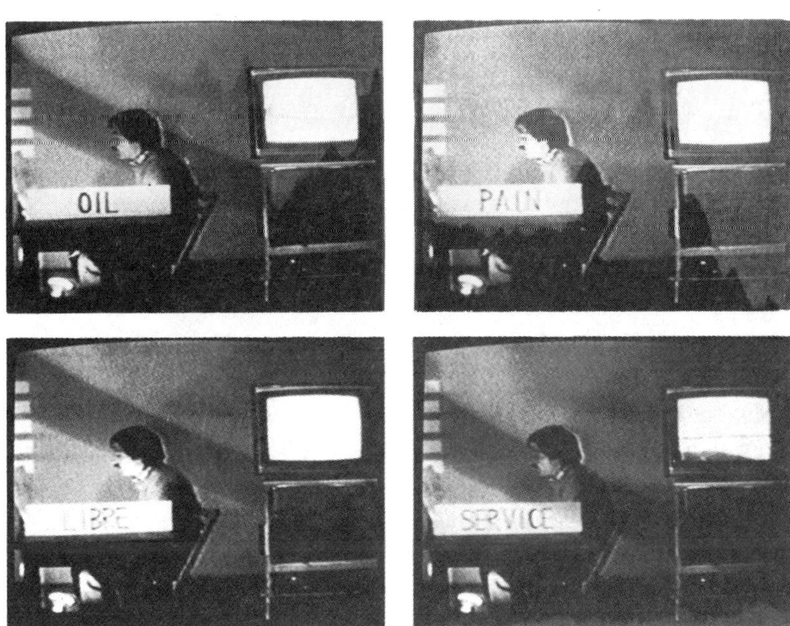

—Tom Konyves, from "Yellow Light Blues," 1979.

Untitled

Claudia Lapp

o animus
everywhere i see you
ever changing triptych
of male beauty
sensitive sensuals
tall-walking and lithe

on my red skateboard
i zoom by you
                    in mukluks
                                    sneakers
                                                sandals
                                                        shoeless

you try and catch my hair
you don't see my trajectory—
skateboard aimed for outer space
                                                    thru inner space
                                                    thru you, Love
                                                    and back again

Feb/79

shoes

Claudia Lapp

she took her black fuck-me shoes
all the way to greece
packed among films & tent
and only wore them once,
in an old patras hotel,
no, twice
once inside the room
and once after

Digging

Claudia Lapp

this rage to dig self
dig up self
get to the bottom of it

i try anything for revelation
    palmistry
        psychodrama
i'm remembering
        how mad i got when they cut my hair
        how i broke a window, said it wasn't me
        how i lorded it over the kids on the block
        how i hated my dolls, mutilated them
        how i loved to be tied up and rolled in blankets
        how the smell of blankets drove me wild

Here/There

Claudia Lapp

that horny afternoon light in patras port hotel
that light of january on top of notre-dame
that saffron leaving paris light inside the taxi cab
that pristine yellow loft light while high on lsd
that sheet-white morning breakfast light in inns of austria
that early rose and blue light on domes of santorini
that foggy all-alone light of massachusetts shore
that horny early-morning light when bodies melt the winter

Shelley

John McAuley

Shelley rules the margin of the Westwind:
Anticyclones, cold wet humans, a brotherhood
Of Clones, birthdays beginning with ice cream,
Strawberry, not Vanilla, galloping horses &
Music for merry-go-rounds, the telekinesis
Of spring, britches without flys,
Boots filled with microscopic stones,
Halos & atoms, Tai Chi as centered
In the Western Belly, straightening legs
& flexible feet.

Lulu

John McAuley

I feel the scars, dear.
Began two letters this A.M. in a lonely
Anatomical hand. My love for you feels like
Somebody cut my tonsils out. Your understanding,
Your encouragement make it possible for me to be honest.
I carry our vows with an inescapable weight
Of destiny trailing behind me. To be exact,
I take kissing to be religious, our tongues move
This way & that ceçi cela, seeing your eyes
A foggy georgian blue, not wanting
To lose the touch of your serif hair,
Not wanting to waste the dark
As the Ark continues.

from *Mattress Testing*

John McAuley

i caress your lips
to elicit the fragrance of peach
i caress your lips
i eat your peach

we are the romantic hungries
we dream of making bacon
we dream up songs for eyes
knowing kissing will be rewarded
in the pear of paradise

i pound my cyrus the great
you waggle your delta wing hips
doors slam
in our brains

•

he could see a short coastline of seduction
for this princess of babylon
this turtledove of invitation
he felt like a missionary
in his wish dream
he could feel himself grow larger
he thought of freud &
his golden book of private parts
poor freud he thought
how he succumbed to cancer of the jaw
victim of twenty cigars a day &
a chronic sub-vocalization process
at any rate
did not freud say
religion begins at our erogenous zones?

from *Divisions*

Stephen Morrissey

••

the things I have failed at
the wind tonight thru the trees
the sound of it in this room
areas of being   spaces
I cld have moved in   met people
been friends   only now
seeing things
                    clearly

o go back to stargazing

walking on beaches   sea shells   a single seagull

the smell of seaweed

there is even there the need to commune even tho

                                                            alone

(the single dark sky
separations of stars from stars
comets from meteors   the big bang theory
& continental drift   we taureans know
the feel of the earth
we lie down on the grass
& feel a rock under the head
as a pillow   it is a good rock
you make friends with that rock
you cant offend it   o happy rock
for a second think of taking it home
& then reconsider   leave it there
& when you leave   / your eyes are moist
at this departure
human society offers nothing   this rock
grows smaller behind you it offers only
its silent goodbye goodbye you have not
failed it you have for a moment dreamt
on its warm surface it now lies there in the sunlight
it will never forget your presence I promise you

(we shld just let
the poem grow

let the mind grow
be passively aware

of its movement   but
watch

as it flowers

sitting on a park bench   beneath some trees
                                        for shade

a woman comes into the park
in her bikini
spreads a blanket on the grass
& lies down

and in another park   10 years later

the percy walters park

I am eating lunch
there are people lying on the grass
enjoying the last days of sun

there is a poem for each month of the year
there is a poem for each week & day
for each hour & second

all time expands into a flower & then
dies

we left the hospital
walking down to ste. catherine street
she talkt continuously for blocks

a few days before
I had gone with you to the hospital
you cried when I left

I went home holding back my tears
all the way & as soon as I got in
the door / cried uncontrollably
for hours

we mustnt leave each other
we must stop while we have
the chance we

must stop killing each other we must

while we can learn to speak

let the words & feelings be flowers

so that they can die & we can die too
die so that we can live be silent
so that we can listen

walking along the beach in ventura
the pier running out into the pacific ocean
islands off the shore
farther south south of
ensenada the beach
was miles of sand
sandpipers running out with
the tide
endless repetitions
of waves sand dollars
found on the beach piles of
heavy white shells

a conch with its spiral shape

& to be alone
by the ocean

to stand by the shore
the sand hot
beneath one's feet

& watch the waves

the ocean   the moon

the constant expansion & contraction

lie down on the beach & watch the clouds
forming on the horizon   forming
into a whiteness over yr head

the sea spray becoming a drop of rain

the poem becomes a written thing

• • •

Montreal, April 1, 2, 4/77

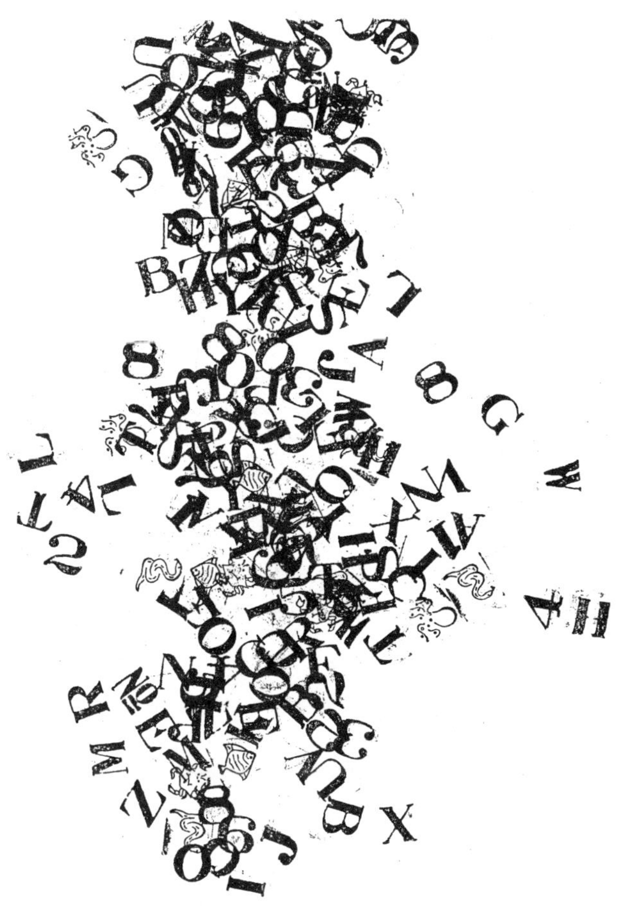

Ode To The Possibilities

Ken Norris

It is as if you've just called from the airport,
are on the way in, and it is the right action
taking place in the wrong year.
What we are having for dinner is questionable;
we know that, in part, it will be each other
but what about all of those other wonderful and terrible
delicacies?
The banquet is spread as are the sheets
of the bed, and I suppose I could say
something about your legs here. Your hair
is curling around the corners of the world.

I can't help but wonder how it could have happened.
Whatever became of junk and yellow taxicabs?
We both like Italian food but it didn't start or stop there.
It lingered in the doorways of the world
and you have woven and won a garland of my love, don't ask
how we have come to this, it is you
who are arriving. I look out the window
and the streets are bright with circumstantial lights.

I've walked along the edge of the river
wondering about the catch the small boats bring in
as they tack their way from shore to shore
zig-zagging against the wind. Have they made it
a good time in the clean waters of upriver?
And now the sun as well as wind catches their sails.

What we make of the night
is all so different from what we make of the day.
Dogs in the street are barking as the sun goes down,
the sky is an absence of purple
having lost all desire to be described.
Stars are gathering force at the filling-station of eternity
and night brings you returning to me
on feet neither winged nor sandalled
but in simple leather shoes.

It's been a thin line you've walked between
things done in the name of romance

and those in the cause of depravity.
I've heard you question the logic of these systems
maybe once. It appeals to you, the automatic service
of this or that always ringing your doorbell.
You rarely test the temperature of water,
the texture or fluidity of anything.
Your body a painter's palette, dabs of pigment
adorn you. Cavalcades of bells
and mysterious late night calls compose a litany
that somehow sings the praises of you.

Artie

Ken Norris

Artie returns with the arrival of summer,
bringing with him a crescent moon
which he plants in the dark blue night sky.
He returns with stories of the West
& a black notebook full of poems
composed on a thousand typewriters. He gives us
poems which we take & turn like jewels in our hands,
they are like stars shining in the warm space
all cynics call a void. He coughs for us
& we begin to relax, he curses a few enemies
& our hearts unfold like flowers that have been
a long time closed. A bit of that foreign shore
is brought to us in the lines of his face.

Al Purdy reading at Véhicule Art Gallery, November 1977.

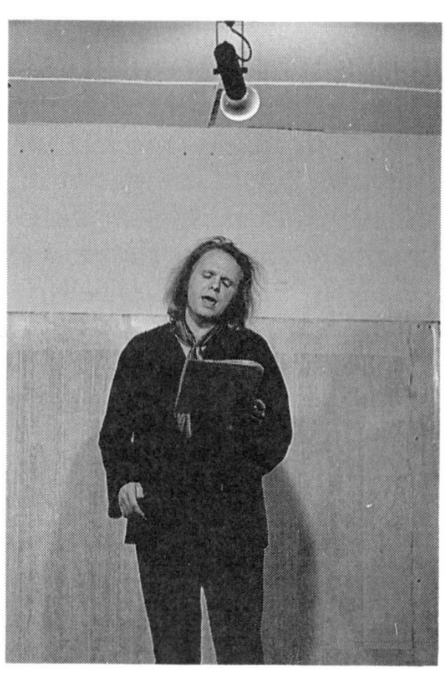

bpNichol reading at Véhicule Art Gallery, February 1978.

bill bissett at Powerhouse Gallery, Fall 1983.

Lionel Kearns at Powerhouse Gallery, Fall 1983.

A Real Good Goosin': Talking Poetics

Maker Press, 1980

Louis Dudek: About all this new Montreal Poetry, the question is whether there are any new critical ideas behind the poetry. Are there any principles behind what you people write, or do you just churn it out without thinking?

Ken Norris: Well, I don't know if you could get everyone to stand under the same umbrella, but all the Vehicule poets are working with a personal aesthetic; that's what varies, the particular approach to the problem. I'd have to say that all of us share certain post-modern biases; the old modernist tension between tradition and innovation is shot, there's no going back, this is the 20th century at last. And in the face of that I'd have to say that all of our work is celebratory, we celebrate what it is about life that we can find to celebrate. Eliot's revulsion in the face of the world/ religious apotheosis is long gone. The Vehicule poets are something new in Montreal because they bring an experimental bias into an essentially conservative town in terms of poetry; and we're a strange wedge/ aberration off the Black Mountain/bissett-Nichol connection because our experimentation is not wide open; although our work has a certain amount of "research," as Steve McCaffery calls his work, there's also a concern for the poem as working entity. I'd also have to say that, although we've tended to emphasize the influence of poets like Bowering and the Black Mountain poets, our influences are really more widespread and at times rather amorphous. We believe in a democracy of "themes" and objects; supermarkets are as important as great cathedrals if you know how to look at them right. Peter Van Toorn sees us as being "messy" rather than "neat" in our writing and, again, I think that's a choice we've made about how to approach the poem and life, though again we do this to varying degrees among the ranks.

Stephen Morrissey: Personally, I just churn it out without thinking and then certain principles appear. But why must we have principles? What do principles have to do with writing poetry? I think that is a backward approach to writing poetry, to have principles first and then write. First you churn it out and then presto you have principles. And then the principles have to be negated or you have the problem of consistency to principles. When are we going to get over this academic dualistic approach to poetry?

Dudek: Aha! So the cat's out of the bag. First, this thing about "aberration from Black Mountain/bissett-Nichol" seems to me a major error now perpetuated beyond the thirty-year mark, i.e. that poetry must be emitted (not *made*), as you breathe (not *think*). Mess is naturally the result. Who will remember the messes? Recently, a project out west, POETRY GOES PUBLIC, has put individual poems on posters. Really fine poems, set off beautifully, with artistic design. This kind of thing can change poetry; it will focus on the perfection of the individual poem, not on the plops, the flops, the pflux. Imagine the poem cut in marble, painted on silk, poured in Monel metal, then you will try to make a poem that's worth this expense of effort. A poem (art) is defined as something that *endures*, while everything else perishes. Look back over history and say where there was poetry; surely not where somebody belched creatively, but where they have left something you can still read. Now this is where Ken's "democracy of themes and objects" is also doubtful: There's a major confusion. There is no democracy of objects. All objects involve negative or positive affect: "bird thou never wert" is opposite to "turd thou never wert." And we make poetry, willy-nilly, out of this polarity. O yes, the "willy-nilly" is Stephen's point: which came first, the theory or the poem? Actually, if the poem just came to Stephen "without thinking," then probably someone else did his thinking for him, and he is just latching on to a line of poetics. It is true, however, that poems "just come"—they'd better not come at all if they don't sometimes just come. But a poet is a man who "has thought deeply," as Wordsworth says. Great periods of poetry usually come just after or just as a new theory has been or is being worked out.

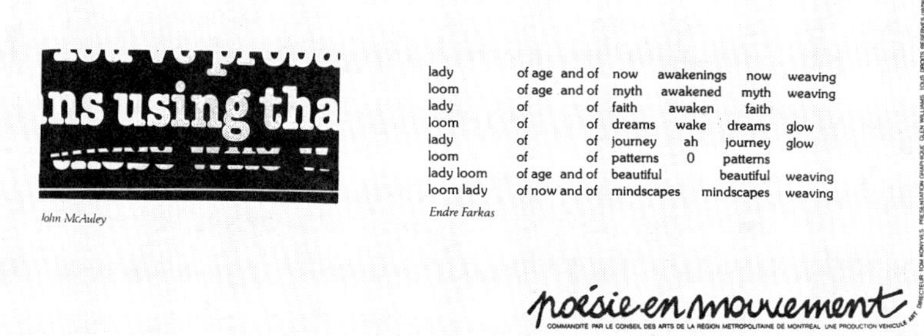

Endre Farkas: First about the "principle vs. the churn": I don't think it is as clear as that, at least not for me. It (the process that eventually is the poem) is constantly at work/play, touching/being touched by images, ideas, lines, flashes, etc. which in turn, turn me on to consider certain *principles*. Other times it's vice versa and other times...

I do not have one unshakeable principle to which I mold my poems. To be a prisoner of one would be to condemn my writing to a uniformity of form, context and deadness.

I partially agree with Steve that the principles of poetry and about life tend to come after the work (sometimes, because poems are revelatory, it happens at the same time). However, I am also aware of the reality that I do formulate principles about writing, but they are not rigid. They tend to be malleable, accommodating ideas that are poems first and principles after.

Wordsworth is right when he says that a poet is a person who has thought deeply, but he should have also said that a poet does not think in a deductive, linear, philosophical manner but more in an intuitive, disjointed-connected manner. At least this has been my experience. And I am convinced that this is a valid "deep thinking" experience.

At this point in my life and work, I feel that I am working the yin/yang world of chaos and focus, taking chances and from those encounters I choose elements and directions. One element is the world of the *everyday*. I often find myself staring at its goings-on with awe. (Thus my appreciation of David McFadden's poetry.) And when I am able to transcribe (not describe) that *awe* into a poem, then the subject can be birds or turds: it don't make no never mind. Blake and the Romantics have taught us that.

And while on the subject of subjects—let's remember that there is a definite difference between subject and theme. One can write about Europe, Vegetables, Murders, Mattress Testing, No Parking & Etc. and definitely not be writing about europe, vegetables, murders, mattress testing, no parking & etc.. . .

I also think that there is only one theme that my poetry deals with (though I do not have this theme consciously on my mind when I write), and it is "the journey." Before I get N. Frye over the head, I must differentiate between "the journey" and "the quest." The quest has been a theme of literature ever since man wanted to know where he was going. It always implies a goal—a holy grail—whereas the journey implies the process, the goal being to be aware of the journey and not considering it a necessary evil to get over. We *know* where we're going to end up. Let's focus on the chaos that is the journey and see what that is. When I write I have no fixed destination but rather try to be open to the moments and visions that the poem reveals to me. "As the breath is the journey / I move…"

Now, about this "messy" business. Peter's remark was not in reference to our lack of care about our craft/the making of the poem, but to our use of the open form. In fact, the so-called "messies" are probably more concerned with form than the "neats" because they are using it as an integral ingredient in the making of the poem, whereas the "neats" are using it as a paint-by-number outline to produce recognizable shapes rather than poems in the sacred sense.

Now, about schools: School's out! Ken is really keen on trying to make a school out of the seven of us who can't even agree on where to eat, let alone on poetics. I grant that we share certain attitudes about writing, but I think they are shared by all good writers everywhere. The seven of us do share a community mindedness that the other English poets in this city do not. I think this stems out of the fact that we put "the making of" before "the making it." And because of public activities, we have been labeled the Vehicule Poets—for better or worse. But we don't have a collective manifesto or an "ism" by which we live, write, or die. This, I think, is to our advantage, as we don't feel hemmed in by a dogma which could limit our growth. It seems to me that "schools" in this country (perhaps elsewhere too) are formed by writers who met in undergraduate/ graduate daze and were being influenced by/rebelling against the same teacher(s). These writers were usually at the *tasting* stages of their careers. We converged *after* our school daze and owed no allegiance to any immediate teacher and when we met we were past *tasting* and in the *probing* stage. There is a definite difference.

We are seven individuals who happen to live and write in Montreal in a language that is of no interest to our own English community… "Poetry is a food that the bourgeoisie—as a class—have been incapable of digesting"—Octavio Paz, nor to the majority of this province or this country. Perhaps because of this, we, in a Canadian context, are seven hermetic poets whose mission is "To give a purer sense to the words to the tribe." And the tribe will remain lost until they come to realize this.

Of course, our hanging out together may have some influence on our writing, but I'm not so sure which came first, our individual attitudes or the collective. The two general areas where I find some similarities are 1) our concentration on the subject of the everyday and in its exploration we map/diagnose/sing/cry about the human condition. Tom may be the exception, but he does use colloquial clichés in ways that give us fresh perspectives about them and their relation to our existence. 2) We tend to be celebratory…out of the realization that we have no choice.

Ken talks about being in the 20th century (21st) and the no-going-back. In my poetry I tend to write about being alive and being very much influenced by this fact. It makes me very aware of the fact that I am alive/ am dying and it is between those two realities that I project my verse/ voice via the imagination.

Are there any new critical ideas behind the poetry?

Well, one of the definitions of poetry that I believe to be true is Wordsworth's "poetry is charged language." From this premise I have gone on to think about and occasionally consciously set out to write what

I call "kinetic" poems. By kinetic I mean a poem that does not rely on "description" nor the word as "symbolic" but rather on language and form(s) that are active (more verbal than adjectival, more tonal than philosophic) and by its charge evokes the real memory in us.

Also, in the last few years, I have become involved with artists (dancers and composers) from other disciplines and working with them I have started to develop "modular" poems. These are "imagistic" short poems whose components can be permutated and this permutation creates echoes that are effective because of their resonance, not their repetition. Working with dancers and composers is also teaching me the important role that time and space have in a poem. This kind of work has given me an appreciation for the poem as a living thing rather than the poem as an artifact. I prefer working within an open form where the boundary is the imagination and not the theory or the past. Because words have meaning—words can never say—but a poem does—and because it is—it moves, and moves us.

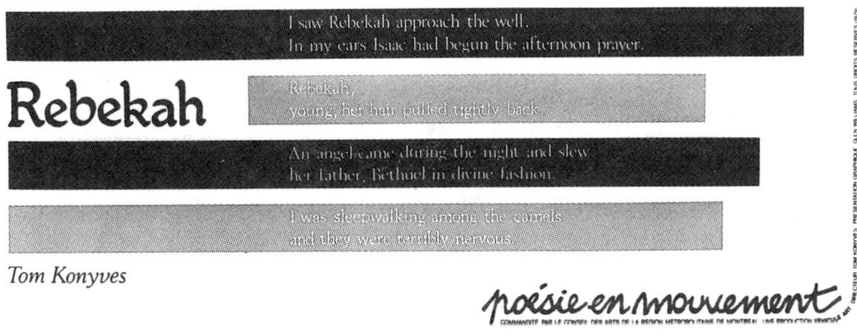

Tom Konyves: To be at the point where the instinctive feel for a thing becomes articulated as "principles"...even the necessity of the question you pose smacks of "which brand of soap do *you* use?"...that there are two attempts in poetry: the timely poems (wherein the style of a generation is held up to ridicule or some other such finger-pointing) and the timeless (a word whose letters have combined in a mystical timeless fashion to fashion a response like "to ease a burthened heart").

...I keep seeing there is no one there. The messianic man-god has not fully come, there are remnants of his garment among us all, his flesh we won't touch till we die, so we reach for the handle, insert the key, give it a turn, a kick and zoom!...it's the vehic(u)le. "What is man" principle in my (our) poems? "What is God" principle "what is life (death)" principle "society" principle.

...or we have thought about it and decided, aw, forget it, it's not worth the hassle, these problems are equally pressing, if we solve *these* perhaps we solve those, too. For myself, I keep seeing there is no one there. It's a dark area of the hall, I carry an evanescent torch. It seems that I either have too much time in my grasp, or not enough. Blake's proverb: "Enough, or Too much" refers to this incentive to writing.

Form and content are the left and right hand playing piano. The principles: Do your deepest desire. Edit those desires. For the deepest desires rarely edify when clothed with words and, moreover, the extent to which contraries abound nullifies any embracing statement which attempts to reveal the untold truth...

...M. Harris in grace: "Life, Death: small things..." once they leave the hand, what do my (these) words do? Visualizations of my inner processes, mostly anti-narrative, i.e. disturbing, disjointed in a careful form, a slow left hand. These words can do anything, I think let us go and find new things in there. We were in a cave of years, some of us, and we are leaving the cave now, our writings are on the wall, now perhaps we will resume our journey on the yellow brick road to a post-modern Oz.

Dudek: Ken Norris traipsed in here today and we began talking about the permanent and the flux. I told him my line "You can't drown in the same river twice"—the flux must end somewhere. He said, "You only disappear from the flux." I'd say it is because he believes there's nothing but change that the poems tend to become ephemeral, no better than any other transitory junk. "What arbitrary rubbish this world is" (Donne). The idea of permanence makes for the idea of permanence in poems.

I like the way you fellows descend into the chaos of the actual. I like your spontaneity. I like your experimental attitudes. I think the new *Postcards* demonstrate a very consistent poetics. Casualness, colloquial speech. The shaping of the ephemeral moment into a significance. They are poems.

Let's get deeper into this. When I write a poem I am entirely different from the man who writes an article or a book review or a report. In a poem the words happen, they just come. I let them. Otherwise I wouldn't write. To interfere with what is happening is to distort the poem. Just a very small degree of intelligence and supervision is necessary. Very tactful. Any revision later that violates the text as it came, that begins rewriting the words, is fake. Is goddamn writing skills. Is an intrusion.

What I despise in other people's poems is goddamn writing skills. What I love is poems that happened. You can smell the difference a mile away.

In other words, there's a word-assembler inside our heads. Under certain states of emotion and disturbance it starts sending out a ticker-tape of words, it goes automatic. Not that it's irrelevant or incoherent. In fact, it's very well organized by its inner causes (whatever they may be) and it is sometimes as rational as Aristotle. But it's from the inner compulsions, and so it's charged with the communicable emotions.

So far, I think you would agree with me. (Or would you?) Anyhow, Ken Norris said that with the permanent (Platonic ideas) one tends to get too far into the stratosphere of the abstract. With the other extreme, right down into the garbage dump of actual life. Why do we have an imagination, that power which is behind the word-assembler of the poet? It is to seek for possible webs of unity, to organize the chaos of impressions, to create an order. That is, a permanence. At least a semblance of permanence.

Isn't this the key? That's what you're doing when you just churn it out—with all those "democratic" anarchic details—is hunt for a touch of solid ground, a point of rest, an affirmation, a glimpse of some permanent good thing? Think it over.

Artie Gold: "Pass..."

John McAuley: Poets by and large are self-educated. In fact, all true education is a form of self-education; the difference between rote learning and natural assimilation is simple: rote learning is based on end gaining. Applying principles to the poetic process encourages end gaining or a kind of intellectual grasping for straws to the detriment of creative awareness. If anything typifies this group, it's our honesty as far as intellectual bullshit is concerned. We don't ass kiss each other or our ideas about poetry.

Obviously, everyone works in a distinct and unique way, but not everyone keeps principles first and foremost in mind while writing. However, I believe in the transmogrification of revision as a strategy to get from virgin manuscript to book or reading draft. As I see it, revision is a byproduct of the invention of writing. Revision simply consolidated expression. I suppose oral poetry remains essentially virgin, though I suspect mnemonic metrics employed by the oral poet lead to concision with repeated voicings.

Black Mountain poetics teach nothing in the way of principles but offer certain working methods which may or may not be used depending on the individual's inclination to formulate his line with respect to tradition. Several of these approaches are: whatever sounds beautiful has poetic buoyancy, therefore, trust the ear; distrust similes for they fall too easily; respect the pun and be sensitive to the narrative acceleration of metaphor.

We took no oaths like lawyers or doctors; yes, our identity is tribal though our markings are invisible. Yet none of us is writing the same kind of lines, our syntactical usage is as varied as our fingerprints. Each of us relies on the evidence of personal exploration rather than on shared principles and we are not writing interchangeable poetry. Louis, some of the things you've been saying sound like a sermonette; as if you are halfway up Mount Sinai exhorting, "create order, create permanence...create a semblance of permanence..." What is this? A short circuited Zen telegram? The seven of us do have one thing in common: we have all worked to keep this city on the poetry map for the past half decade or so, organizing readings, doing magazines, setting up presses, and distributing books. We have been keeping things going, we haven't been building monuments to ourselves.

I am a churner; what a fine powerful word "churning" is—sexual. Almost breeds by itself, indicates sleeve rolling and perspiration, the actual working exploration. The breath is indeed important as tone leader of the narrative; using the breath keeps the ears open, liberates awareness, gives a topos to language as primum materia; using the breath gives the poet a first-rate kinesthetic tool. I remember the first time I discovered this one night eight years ago; I was baking bacon and onion bread, reading Bowering's *The Gangs of Kosmos* and wanting the book to go on and on, turning the pages, feeling as if my fingers had eyes.

You see, following the breath is natural, as it carries the seeds of necessary inhibition: defined correctly by John Dewey and F.M. Alexander. Inhibition is the key to all integrative self-education and creative activity. Louis, I think your statement about the "error" of Black Mountain not only stinks with historicism, it also exposes a certain partiality on your part for poetry predetermined by the authority of principles.

Principles don't create poets, smart genes do; I'm not fooling, smart genes violate Mendel's Laws of Selection and explain why poets are born not made.

Churning is nothing like uttering spurious coinage; it is the stitching of words across the page with the rapidity of a table tennis game between the People's Republic of China and Taiwan. Churning involves a recentering of the consciousness into the hand from the mobile of the arm. The Surrealists were aware of this; Desnos and Breton were churners of the first water. However, their churning was a random, almost occult ideomotor technique, without the inhibitory guidance of the breath, and that's the distinction between automatic writing and true poetic exploration. The unpredictability of churning, the very going where one knows not, is exhilarating. The old Friar Eliot pose is tiresome and boring. Churners represent a chorus of bullfrogs in Walden Pond. Churning should not be some kind of mark of Cain, neither should be experimentation, though both seem to be dirty words in Canada.

Resurrect the bones of Bliss Carman or Wilson MacDonald and I'm positive you could draw SRO crowds; Canadian conservatism makes me sick; if this was Minneapolis rather than Montreal, we would get more respect.

There is a long history to fast writing. Thomas Heywood wrote 250 plays at the hazy height of the English Renaissance. He was a churner, he knew thinking takes care of itself. Daniel Defoe's *Robinson Crusoe* is probably the most popular book of all time, but Defoe's success didn't stop him from churning out hundreds of books; what about Samuel Johnson? Anton Chekov is another example of a furiously creative artist who made good. There is something sublime, forceful and obvious to the craft of churning which is not the thinking of words and the writing of them; it is the writing and the writing of them.

All is fair in love and poetry. You won't find me coming to the poem with principles dropped on the table like a stake of pretty coloured chips. I am ready to palm wild cards and aces and I'm not going to worry about it one bit. Principles in relation to poetry are optional, like suspenders which may hold up a pair of pants, but they aren't wearing. Kowtowing to principles has destroyed more poets than Plato could have ever hoped for.

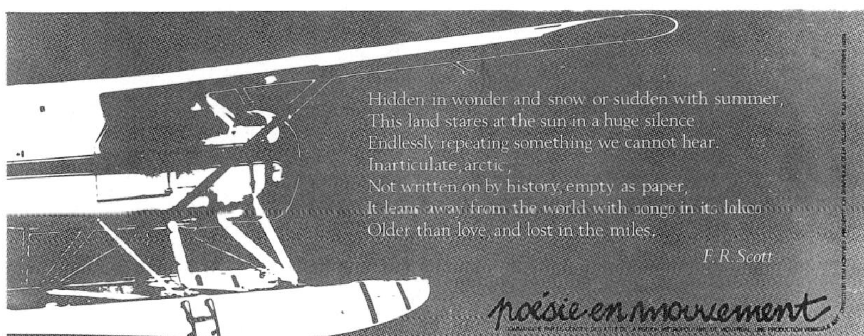

Claudia Lapp: Well, first, this is hard for me because i want this to be a letter to you all on Everything 'n i'm 'sposed to stick to Poetry. Second, it's been two and a half months since i walked along Sherbrooke Street. By now, i have some perspective vis à vis you Montreal poetry *kalyanamitras* (Sanskrit—it means "spiritual friends"—'n you all *are*). Looking back, without knowing for certain just where you all are at, but having a feeling of it from our April recording session and scattered conversations before i left—what was/is most precious for me was the atmosphere of encouragement and support and tolerance of diversity in Montreal—and knowing that something was always *brewing* with us, that we were all churning and channeling and receiving and sharing. The form wasn't as important as our aspiration to evolve, to keep moving, not to get stuck at a comfortable place just because we got good at it (how we've changed our *ways* over the eight or nine years we've been together, how we're still working to uncover-recover our Voices: Ken hasn't remained a Vegetables poet, Tom won't be a dadaist forever, my fantasies have become something else by now, etc. Our poem-ing a yoga in which we worked out our demons (or should I use *daimons*—that includes light and darkness). In that creative emerg-ency, which took the form of poem of videotape or performance or song, we express the demon-daimons of all hu-mans. We move-d alone, or collectively, often sympathetic to each other's blockages and neuroses (but not coddling them). We saw when we could act together, and when we had to be on our own (free from influences)—I liked that we helped one another but didn't smother each other!

9/16/79 suite…in August one night i'd leapt outta bed w/ an idea of what to write for this linked letter (*great* idea) and it was essentially a list—of "masters" of making—and it's important to list 'em because they corona me at all times (we poets being a part of a chain of intense *transmitters*— "timeless" TK "poems that happen" LD…so here goes: Basho, Issa, Sappho (all thru translation, alas). Holderlin, Rimbaud, German Volkslied; e.e. cummings, W.C. Williams (esp. Paterson), Emily Dickinson, Ginsberg (last seen in Toronto using Australian song stick, singing Blake and Mexican City Blues on Harmonium), Robert Bly (singing Kabir and his own verse on dulcimer), Kabir, Rumi, Tagore, Richard Sommer (esp. for left hand poems), Penny Kemp, Anne Waldman, Daphne Marlatt, Gary Snyder, Kavafy (again in translation)— I'm cutting myself off here, the list's too long!

Other *keynotes*: Troubadors MUSIC ("Respect the ear/De la musique avant toute chose"). Ballads, blues, Middle English Cards, square dance callers, auctioneers melody-ing here in Appalachia are very much in my consciousness. Working on using dulcimer for my own songs and chants (a singer said to me the other day, once member of a fine group, "Trapezoid," the key to "*Memory* is music…you can sing forty-three verses with ease, but without the music to carry you, it's impossible.")

Listening to the "new" Joni Mitchell (what a far-reaching Voice and Spirit), who's mingled w/ Mingus, I said to myself—Yeah, now she's evolving her poetry, really using the music that's all around her, and all this while being a Superstar (whose times are numbered, I hope—I mean, we can't afford to feed the Superstars forever…more important planetary work to be done.)

CELEBRATION—well, that's always been my poetic stance (doesn't only mean sensation-al/erotic). At thirty-three, it becomes something else as well. Poems that heal (make whole) on a collective level. Poet as shaman/ecologist (Snyder).

POEMS THAT HAPPEN are the only ones I really care about now. They come from beyond wanting them. Your whole life being is a preparation for them. They're clear, authentic, often timeless. The following, from a Rosicrucian book, really says it about Song and Who we poets are (Yeats would agree!):

In songs "the words of poetic sentences and the notes of musical phrases are blended into a strange magical alchemy by which the poetic word is intensified and the musical idea is made concrete. Since tone is the archetype of sound and words are sequences of composited sounds, the art of song is seen to be the archetype of poetic reading. The great singer...perceives intuitionally the musical value inherent in the literary text and fuses these." And "All creative artists are mediators between the divine and human." (Human: "Divine Mind)

More to follow... Love to you all, Claudia

Dudek: Words words words. Beware that we don't trip ourselves up on the mere words. McAuley writing against "principles" demonstrates principles—his reply is full of ideas about writing, the right kind of writing. That's all I mean by "principles." The same is true about every other contribution here (except Artie Gold's "Pass"), they show what's behind your poetry...

But to continue my sermonette, I see two parts of the writing process: a) the writing it down, and b) the working it up. Spontaneous expression, and then revision—but going a littler further than John McAuley on revision. He says it "consolidates express." OK. But I would say this: a poet with a lot of gift will pour out rich raw material (see Claudia Lapp's statement just above). As the great Marianne said, if you want "the raw material of poetry in/all its rawness" then "you are interested in poetry." But you may be interested in poetry and perish among the junk-heaps and slag-heaps of forgotten versifiers. What is required to turn your talent into that real poetry you are interested in is the critical sense, discrimination, a grasp of "principles" which will make your revision masterful. Who was that character in Maugham's *Of Human Bondage* who thought of himself as a great artist and never did a bloody thing? Henshaw, I think. Remember Henshaw, Henshaw remember (if I remember him rightly); i.e. if a writer knows the difference between a good line and a bad one, a good phrase and a bad one, a good combination and a lousy mess, then he can revise, and he can make a poem out of his emissions, or missions. In other words, to be a good reviser, you've got to know, to think, to read a lot. After the churning, you've got to "pull" the toffee. But hell, maybe we've exhausted this one. The purpose is to see what people think. I am impressed that there is a lot of consensus among your group, despite your denying that there is any. The fact is, a lot of people working together, in a time and a place, cannot help but be similar in ways they do not even realize. The critic will see this. The real problem is your relation to the society around you. Most of you deny having any audience. And there's the bigger political question in all this, the way that your poetry is steered by the relation you have to the world around you. You say you "celebrate"; but you actually kibbitz, i.e. you are spoilers, anarchists, outsiders. There's your political dilemma (by the way, I'm reading this good book, Gerald Graff, *Literature Against Itself*, which has a lot to say about this kind of postmodernism). How about going into postmodernism?

Norris: Having never been an extensive reviser, I think I'll just let that one roll by me, and actually that point *has* probably been beaten to death, or at least discussed at length by you and McAuley. I talked to Tom before and asked him if he thought that we were really "spoilers, anarchists, outsiders" and he said "Sure," so I guess I won't even argue with that too much. I *try* to celebrate life in my poetry, even if there are things I have criticisms of. I recently saw a quote of Purdy's somewhere in which he said something to the effect that "All poems are love poems" and that's an idea that I've always carried around myself, feeling that to write poetry requires a real act of love, that feelings of love are the only things that get poets moving.

But to get on to the more pressing question of "postmodernism" or where all of this fits in, what's going on in the writing. I think it's important to talk about the writing itself after having hashed over so many pages of principles. I'm not as committed as you are, Louis, to a poetry of permanence: in fact, I'm quite suspicious of poetry that's made with permanence in mind. It has the smell of the academy. A recent thought of mine is that Art is short for artificial and that isn't a notion that really appeals to me. You yourself have always strived for a poetry that would wed life and art. I also remember talking in the past to you, suggesting that there's nothing real about realism. It *is* all artifice, I suppose, but that's something I'm not really willing to admit to, and a lot of my energy in writing these days is aimed towards defeating the imperialism of art. I suppose that's also reflected in the Graff book as an element of postmodernism.

But to move on to the writing at hand, I am really excited by the writing that I'm seeing going on around me, the potentiality I see in it. I know this is probably going to raise some hackles, even among the members of the group (if Artie will allow me to say that there *is* one), but I'm just now starting to see a real possibility for something new, a new phase, a real postmodernism.

And it'll be something that isn't a further elaboration off of Modernism, rather something that runs counter, that takes us out of aesthetic dead ends. For a long time I've been looking at post-World War II poetry, Black Mountain, the *Tish* guys, bpNichol, as postmodern, but I'm starting to realize that it's just been a convenient way of talking about Modernism's later stage, and to call it "post" is to take into account the changes and shifts. But so much of it is really just a continuation of Modernism and, in Canada, catching up with the elements the guys in the 20s and 40s missed, that's the 60s. Interesting stuff like Bowering's *A Short Sad Book*, Nichol's *Alpha Beth Book*, Steve McCaffery's language texts, all that investigation of the medium, that's Modernism. I'm not so sure about bp's *Martyrology*; something significant is going on in that, there's the seed of something. And I see other things starting to bubble up, some among us, others out there somewhere. It's something totally new, and right now we're caught in the last stages of transition. And that's a sign to me of something important happening, a writer in transition, just stepping off from what's become the safe ground of the 20th century, the investigation of the medium, into something else. That's why I get so excited about David McFadden's work; he's come out of the 60s group and constantly been evolving till he's finally, I think, hitting it. *The Poet's Progress* and *I Don't Know* are real transitional works, the last gasps of an old poetry falling away with the seed of something new contained in it which finally blossoms in *A New Romance*, which I think is one of the first bona fide postmodern poems in existence. Although we see guys like Williams kind of pushing it around, I think Pound actually *got* the hard classicism he wanted, but what a classicism, broken images, jagged reality. There's been a real hardness, dryness, a real cutting edge to that, the cutting edge of reality. I think something running counter to that is finally starting to make its presence felt, and I'm afraid to say that it's bringing some of the impulses of romanticism back with it, but it's true. I think further fragmentation in the arts is just the death rattle of Modernism. And the impersonality of Modernism has also got to go, Eliot's platinum plate catalyzing the formation of acid. That's why I'm currently starting to see an essay such as O'Hara's "Personism: A Manifesto" as representing more of an accurate and real direction than Olson's "Projective Verse" essay. And O'Hara seems to me to be more of a lead into the area where we should be going than Olson, even though, as O'Hara suggests, what he's doing may just lead us to the end of literature. Anyway, wandering back, I think there's a real possibility for that something new in the work of some of us. I really see it in Stephen's work. *Divisions* is a kind of working through; those last few pages, to me, point in the direction of a new poetry. Artie, in his new intimacy and in the motive power of the heart in *before Romantic Words*, is pushing up against the gates of something really significant. I suppose I'm beginning to see an organizing principle of coherency in this work, even if it's just a willingness to submit to the mystery or to the forces of life.

It was really important for me to write that poem "MacIvors Point" and to realize that even if I couldn't bring a new measure into being, I could finally see the absolute limitation of the world of particulars. I see Stephen's *Divisions* working through sensibility as its working through life, and I see that going on in my own *Report. Divisions* and *The Book of Fall* (book two of *Report*) both stem out of the same place and they share that incredible degree of intimacy and confessionalism. Stephen succeeds where I fail, however; he at least gets to the point where "the poem becomes a written thing," while I'm still wandering around blinded by the reality of the blank page. But I think by book three I'm finally starting to walk out into something. It's a—no it's not—I was going to say that it's a different world than the one we come up against at the end of *Divisions*, but it's not. Both of us wind up confronting the ocean; in fact, it's where you dropped us off in *Atlantis*, Louis. Stephen gives us:

& to be alone
          by the ocean
to stand by the shore
      the sand hot
              beneath one's feet
& watch the waves
          the ocean   the moon
the constant expansion & contraction
lie down on the beach & watch the clouds
forming on the horizon   forming
into a whiteness over yr head
the sea spray becoming a drop of rain
the poem becomes a written thing

In the last section of book three I come up with *cold* sand, the moon, the ocean, also a lighthouse thrown in for good measure, but I drop us off with this:

The ocean is peaceful tonight
there's not a cloud in the sky,
nature has perfected itself
in a moment that's occupying your senses,
and you have become the perfect lens
for the world to look through
in order to be able to see itself.

Stephen gives us those two beautiful object transformations, the sea spray becoming a drop of rain, the poem becomes a written thing, and I transform subject into object, self becoming lens, the self as totally transparent and clear and something to look *through*, rather than *at*. And all this I see as being somewhere totally different from the perceptive self or the proprioceptive self. And whether anybody else gives a damn, *this* excites me. And to move on, Tom's work is quite incredible in its recognitions. Beyond the nihilism, the surrealism, the dadaism, there are a couple of key insights and, I would suggest, affirmations. That crazy poem of his "Words Can Never Say" embodies a key problem in its title and after that he can write anything to prove his point, which he does. And whether or not you like the tricks and rhythms of "No Parking," the absolute realization of being "in the middle of things" I think is tremendous. These are the things that immediately strike me. I haven't really gotten a handle on specific things I can point to in Endre, Claudia and John at the moment, though the significant work has started to show: Endre's *Murders* is more than just an interesting stroll through the detective genre, I haven't really come to grips with it yet, Claudia's eroticism just knocks me out and I'm really taken with her poem "The Cosmic Hooker," and John's *Mattress Testing* is one of my favourite all-time books of poetry. Where I think we're blowing it right now is simply by still being in transition. There are still the old influences to get clear of, and a few personal awkwardnesses to overcome, but I'm really starting to believe in the significance of the work and the incredible possibilities of breaking new ground. By 1977 I felt like we all finally knew how to write, i.e. could get out a good poem, although we always could backslide into writing something really bad; by now, the end of 1979, I'm beginning to see what I think is important work being done and I'm stunned by what *could* happen in anybody's work at any time.

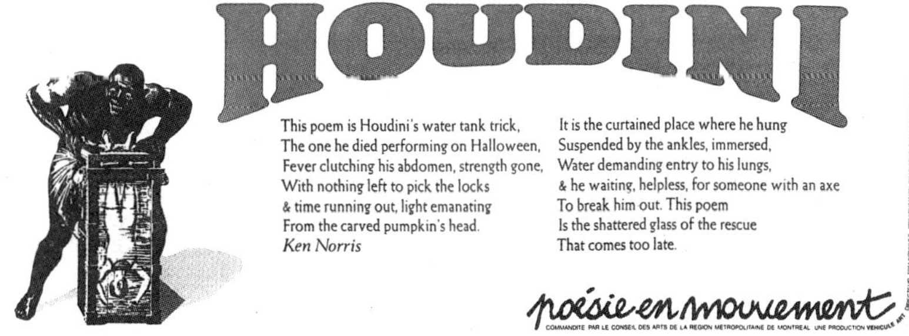

Farkas: Before we rush into the streets declaring ourselves to be the new postmodern poets of Canada, we should first locate ourselves and find out what street we're on and what we are and how we got there and what we are doing there.

Something has been/is happening and I think we are a vital part of it, but I am not sure if we are aware of our role. Investigation and analysis are essential but not because of the vote result, rather because we must understand how we, the important English writers, have coped, survived and flourished in conditions in which the opposite is expected. You know, we just might be the way for the new English-Quebecker. It is in this light that I want to discuss "postmodernism."

In our intro to *Montreal English Poetry of the Seventies* Ken and I said that the English writer in Quebec doesn't have an audience and to write in English is to commit a political act. I still feel very strongly about those statements but feel that they need elaborating, especially the relationship between minority rule, the means and manner of that rule and how they affect the role of the artist in that community.

Prelude
—The New World/Canada was discovered by accident and developed solely for the profit of various colonial powers
—The ownership of Canada was decided on Abraham's field between England and France
—In wars, spoils go to the victor
—The French military, administration and the rich go home, leaving behind the majority of poor French
—The new colonial power replaces the old and sets up its version of the minority ruling group/military/bureaucrats/business

Thus begins the minority's political and economic rule.

It is important to remember that this ruling group was very much apart form the majority of English. However, because of its power, it claimed to speak for the English community. They appointed themselves moral guardians, trendsetters and cultural dictators. And in cultural matters, they followed their business aesthetics: they favoured the bought, the imported, the safe and familiar. Their models were from out there. Conversely, anything made here was not considered desirable for the very same reasons.

In the English milieu, in Montreal, the first "poetic" voices of dissent came from within this ruling class itself: Scott and Smith. They also looked to other places for inspiration and direction but for different reasons: they saw the worthlessness of the examples being offered up by the ruling minority as desirable culture.

Scott and Smith got turned on to the modernist influence of Pound and Eliot. They incorporated these influences into their poems of satire which were directed against the rich exploiters. But *the rich* were a faceless abstract, as were *the poor*. Neither Scott nor Smith dealt with the reality that was at the heart of the matter, the issue of minority rule. This may have been because both Scott and Smith had come out of that minority.

Klein, on the other hand, did not. His immigrant background ensured him of a more intimate involvement, and maybe because of his Talmudic influences he was more sympathetic to the French-Canadian's aspiration on the individual and cultural level. In *The Rocking Chair* he writes in an empathic tone about their history, their politics and their modernization of Quebec. He saw the exploitative process destroying their culture and this is what he lamented. He saw industrialization as the problem and maybe because of his English affiliation he, too, could not focus on the real issue of minority rule. The following generation focused on new poetics and new realities. Dudek, Layton, Souster have working class backgrounds. Their political concerns seem to have been the workers' movement: solidarity/comrades building a workers' paradise on earth and social satire about urban problems. I don't see "minority rule" being an issue. Louis, maybe you can respond to this.

As for us, we didn't know any other way to look at it but as majority rule. We were very acutely aware of that, but I don't think that it was our previous generation of writers who made us aware. It was our francophone contemporains and common sense. The bitch that we inherited was that we didn't have an audience. Not at home, anyway. That's always the case with the new, innovative and interesting, but when there is nothing there before and out of it comes readings, literary presses and books and these things are still ignored, then I wonder. We and the majority of the English have very little in common. We have very little to say to them that would please them, make them comfortable, or allow them to continue living their illusion. This illusion has been shattered for good. The ruling group, as a concept, has moved, and with it so has the bought culture. With this leaving, the falseness of the desired culture was revealed and caused panic and chaos.

One of the essential ways that a people gets to know itself, articulate its fears and aspirations, and name itself, is through its art. We have seen the importance of this relationship both as idea and as reality in the francophone-Québecois society. Here the artists (writers especially) have been in the avant garde and have been a true mirror to their society. The francophone-Québecois culture couldn't have developed without facing up to its minority position in a North American reality but by refusing to live only by that definition. The English writers in Quebec operate out of a similar awareness. This is partly because we recognize that we have more in common with the francophone-Québecois than with the English in Canada-North America. We don't deny our larger world, but know that it is from here that we are working to out there, not vice versa. The new English-Quebecker is beginning to realize this. And he must start to look at the local work of local artists seriously, to look into their mirrors, not to separate himself from the rest of Quebec, but to identify himself within it.

Our audience is awake now and we owe our contemporains much thanks.

Dudek: Very interesting. In fact, you all fascinate me. But can we get on a bit to the actual technics of poetry? What ideas do you have about rhythm, layout on the page, shape? Personally, I think that rhythm is your own identity, it is the way you shake the words out—as different from anybody else. Recently I noted in my book: "Style is the gimmickry." But that is critical of the many styles of modernism, especially in the novel. Real style is not gimmickry, but soul-rhythm. My advice to the young poet is "Start to babble, go into the lalling stage of infancy again, make long strings of internal monologue...then try to throw them into lines on the page...improvise unpublishable private dribble...open the sluice gates of the verbal black box...discover the full powers of the language centers of the mind, in relation to emotion, to sex, to vision, to smell, to touch, to memory, to fear and desire and expectation..." Some bits of this may actually be poetry. But just bits. Don't publish this stuff. Take out the bits that look promising—and start working on them. But now, as you work, remember that the rhythm is sacred, it is the message. Lay it out on the page to preserve the rhythm, and to intensify it. Here, I believe every poet tends to develop, over the years, a secret system of his own. We don't need to discuss this. You either lay down the lines as they are rhythm'd—to interfere is sometimes trivial—or you obstruct the natural rhythm by line endings and breaks, to intensify the rhythm (this has to be done with care), and you work toward a final satisfying shape. (If you don't do this final shaping and polishing, frankly, I am not interested in your work—and nobody else will be interested in the end.) How about the *sound*? Do you want to work for "special effects" of sound? Ralph Gustafson, following G.M. Hopkins, puts all the stress on sound-values—"otherwise it might just as well be prose," he says (see last week's *Globe & Mail*, Dec. 8/79). Perhaps this is true for some poets. It wasn't necessary for the Sermon on the Mount, so far as I know. Perhaps it depends on what you have to say. My own conviction is that when you come to the heart of poetry, or great meaning, the language simplifies. At other times, wandering in the dark wood—or playing marbles—you can make a certain amount of noise for its own sake. As for the *shape*, it is the sense of a completed form, of a new form, of a lovely shape in the air—like good pottery (if you cannot tell when a vase has a good shape, nobody can help you). Recognizing, or making a good form is part of the gift of poetry. Let's recognize, too, that the gift of doing all these things is either there or it is not there; and it is either great or it is moderate: we can only use as much gift as we have.

Konyves: Where, if anywhere, does our poetry differ from the poetry written in the 40s, 50s, 60s? The phenomenon of "Vehicule poetry," as far as I see it, is largely due to the nature of the center of our activities (as group), i.e. the Gallery. For those who became disenchanted with the administration of Véhicule Art, any reference to the "space" arouses anger, frustration, ill feeling. Nevertheless, my experience locates us, if not at the center, on the fringe of experimentation, the calling card of Véhicule Art. The first poets of the gallery, Artie and Claudia, may have thought of the gallery as "free space" for readings, as did the second generation, Endre, Stephen, John. My point is that no matter what we all expected from the gallery in terms of "free space," we received more. We couldn't have walked in the rain and not got wet. We did not meet in a library, we did not get to know one another in classrooms or bars. While the poets read, I believe, "free-form" visual and plastic art hung on the walls, suspended from the ceiling, spread out on the floor, documented with leaflets lying about on ledges next to poetry books we were selling—the new art began flowing through our veins, more or less.

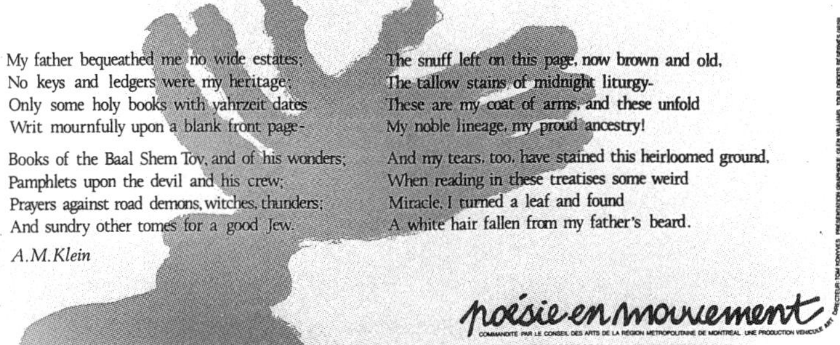

In other words, the decisions we were making in our poems, where to put what, was, to some extent, affected by what we were seeing around us—literally, our visual influences, the poetry of postmodern art.

Therefore, the technics can be partially attributed to new-art making: collage, mixed-media, dissonance, minimalism... What appeals to me most is that we began writing art, not literature. We have all written poems that look and speak like poems written by almost anyone in the English-speaking world. But we have also written poems that could *not* have been written by anyone else, anywhere else. These are the poems poured into the crucible of art, with words; these are the poems painted and layered onto unique surfaces, with words; these are the poems sung, with words; these are the poems spoken by many voices in dialogue; these are the poems that remain silent, beyond words. Ken's poem entitled "Poetry" ends "Plain trickery/This thing we call/Art."

Playing AT JACKS—The Argument

A ndre mesmerized the sound of it
T om visualized it
J ohn-john collaged it, on paper.
A rtie passed. He read it, staring down.

C laudia celebrated it.
K en liked it, didn't like it, etc.
S tephen initiated it.
What is it?

The question is: the depth and (2) journey. The depth is the degree to which the poet is aware of the rhythm of his "soul." (Why do poets date some poems?) Aware of the rhythm of his soul while composing the poem. "Oh good foolishness," cries Artie, in his poem "V." For while we sit here, cozy in the womb-talk of poetry...a man somewhere slips and falls and you know how a certain pain in the ribs can outlast a winter. In my poems, I can't forget what a myriad of wondrous shapes surround the little poem, so words begin to search out different associations from the ones necessitated by their syntax. The poem, as vehicle, becomes jet-propelled (when it works).

Before I wrote the video-poem "Sympathies of War," I wrote the line, "Words magically happily dance between the curtains of stop." I churned it out. Then I recognized the principle. In "Sympathies," the form became "words between the curtains of stop." It was to be more than a mere telegraph poem. Stopping, the cessation of motion, reduction to zero, etc., was becoming the "world of the poem," a good reflection of (or metaphor for) the myriad of coexisting forces revolving about the narrative, what you call "great meaning" and "simplified language." For me, great meaning was nothing without "little meaning" at its side. Endre would understand this in terms of "negative space," the Zen of "what is not there is as important as what is." Giving life to the paper the poem is written on. The power of "nothingness," which gives dimension to "somethingness" or existence. (In one of the issues of *mouse eggs*, our mimeographed magazine, I wrote a poem called "Poem By Ditto," permitting the very paper were using to "speak.")

The danger of all this is that if there's too much "little meaning" and not enough "great meaning," the poem does not work. Too much darkness vs. too little light, etc.

Therefore, the depth of "Sympathies of War" was achieved with "curtains of stop." These were the means of drilling. The matter (the drill) was even more complicated. Using a Hebrew dictionary (specially designed to refer to Talmudic passages), I discovered that there were no less than seven (!) different ways of saying "stop." I began to gather the imagery offered by this text and proceeded to compose the poem, using the dual method of narrative/found poem.

The means of drilling is the form. The drill is the content.

The journey of the poem is a significant concern to all of us. Endre astutely differentiates it from the "quest," implying it's the how, not the what. Perhaps this is the point where we and you differ, Louis. The how is the principle of having no principles (Tzara). It is the poetry for poetry's sake. It is the celebration of the form, the new form.

Morrissey: I feel that form (and by extension, all poetry) is closely connected with being, with the attempt to express the truth of one's being. The difficulty is that we are always changing and therefore one style, one form, isn't adequate. I see my own poetry moving through a variety of forms, clusters of expressions of being. Isadora Duncan writes: "My art is just an effort to express the truth of my Being... It has taken me long years to find even one absolutely true movement."

Where form was a revelation in my own work was in writing the poem "Divisions." I tried to write that poem for ten years; the material was there, but the form wasn't. And without the form, the vehicle for carrying the content was absent. A number of things coincided to allow the writing of the poem. One of those was reading the work of Clayton Eshleman, whose early poems I had been reading and identifying with. Finally the poem was written in a three-day period, and the finished poem required very little editing. "Divisions" was a turning point for my writing. Now I could write something that was true to my being and not reject it two days or two months later, as had been my experience. "Divisions" was a great liberating leap forward for me personally; I felt free of the past, for the past had at last assumed a form through poetry that I was able to deal with, rather than the amorphous mass of confusion that had previously existed.

I agree with Ken Norris that "art is artifice" but it is also a spiritual exercise, or can be; it is my way of understanding my life, and there is nothing artificial about that. Without form there is no poetry, but form should ideally be invented coincidentally with content. Without thinking things over, creating a foundation for one's work, then form is an empty vehicle, a writing that is stylistically pretty but otherwise empty and meaningless.

After writing "Divisions" I wrote long poems for several years; there is a spaciousness to the long poems that seems almost a part of this country. The open spaces, the fact that the land is uninhabited in many areas. However, there is also a spaciousness in the haiku form and it was through writing haikus and concrete poems that I feel I taught myself how to write. I suppose the form of "Divisions" is close to Olson's projective verse, at least it *looks* that way, "looks" because I have not yet studied Olson's work thoroughly. In my other work I have found the two-line stanza, which is really a development for me from haiku, very easy to work with; it has an openness (spaciousness) that seems to move complementary to the content of the poem; that complementary aspect of form and content is essential.

I try to use form as notation indicating how the poem should be read (either silently or aloud). This also brings in Pound's "musical phrase," the music of the poem, the meter. I agree that "rhythm is your own identity" and that "real style is...soul rhythm." At this point, much of my work is a kind of free-form improvisation, writing a lot and then, as Tom Konyves says, "finding the poem in the poem." There must be a spaciousness of being, an openness of being; without that I don't think any poetry is possible. That spaciousness comes across in the poem. It is the open mind and the caring heart behind the poem. The form reveals and is part of these qualities. So any rigidity, any preconceptions about writing are really superfluous and detrimental to writing. For me, writing has become a spiritual exercise in which form is a revelation of being. The poems must come spontaneously, and thus form is the appearance of that spontaneity; the poem must scan well, read well. I agree with Keats when he writes "That if poetry comes not as naturally as the leaves to a tree, it had better not come at all."

If I may return (however reluctantly) to the discussion of principles for a moment, there is one principle that I do follow, and that is to never censor myself when I am writing. There is enough censorship without it being added to poetry. Our burden today is self-consciousness and I feel that poetry is one place where we can begin to free ourselves of this. My objection to principles, again, was based on the fact that whenever principles become preconceptions and rules, then poetry begins to atrophy. Just as poetry atrophies when form indicates a preconceived and recognized way of writing "poetry." This is the death of poetry. In reading what others have said, I can see that we are riddled with principles, but then, why not? We wouldn't be human if we didn't have ideas, beliefs, preconceptions. The difficult thing is not to rest there, but to continue to explore and investigate and feel and think. Today most people's thinking has been done by other people. This is a failing of the school system; the schools do not teach people how to think for themselves; we have become second-hand people. (Wasn't it T.E. Hulme who said that most people's original thoughts would fill about half a page?) But this is in part why I write poetry (not only because I love to sit and write and find a great joy in the act of writing): it is to lay a foundation, to create myself, to create a new form of living that can move sanely and wholly through this life.

Dudek: Dear friends, this is just to say that I've enjoyed carrying on this dialogue with you, and in closing, to thank you for coming out so frankly and for putting this conversation on record. Also, I want to apologize a bit for being professorial and didactic at times—it's a habit of thirty years that's hard to shake, but you've been very tolerant.

Most of all, I want to round it out by saying how I now see your poetry much more clearly. The word for everything—made clear in the last two statements, by Tom Konyves and Stephen Morrissey—is openness. Your poetry, your attitude to life, your feeling for each other—and even for oldies like myself—is open, free, welcoming all possibilities. (In this, like Frank Davey's Preface in the general guide *From There to Here.*) In the poem, especially, this is an aesthetic that needs to be understood. You do not want the poem contained in a structure. You want the structure, so far as it emerges, to correspond and somehow to grow out of that openness to many-sided experience, that sense of the world as an open continuum, and that strange inwardness which moves out of infinite possibility into multiple reality. The poem as a symbol or representation of this open state—often with comic or slipshod effects—is really a projected image of modern reality and consciousness. I believe something similar is happening in Toronto and Vancouver, and perhaps elsewhere, with a local difference wherever poets breathe a different air. A wonderful compilation of this kind of poetry is *The Body*, which just came to me the other day, brought out on the West Coast by Tatlow House. (Obviously, people like McFadden, bissett, Nichol are doing something similar in their way in the Toronto area (the double number of *Impulse* in 1974, Vol. 3, No. 3-4, was a good cross-section.) The public hasn't yet understood what this new poetry is about. We need critics who will do a little explaining and defining, maybe even praising, since a lot of the poetry is already available. (See *The Long Poem Anthology* edited by Michael Ondaatje.) Perhaps then discrimination and enjoyment on the part of a bigger public will follow.

A rivederci.

January 9, 1979-April 15, 1980

Most of the Vehicule Poets at Ste. Anne de Bellevue, Summer 1978.

Left to right: Ken Norris, Endre Farkas, Stephen Morrissey, Tom Konyves, Rupert Van Wyck, Opal L. Nations, Tom Ezzy.

The Insecurity of Art: 5 Statements
Stephen Morrissey
The Trees of Unknowing, 1978

1.

a challenge exists in life & art and that is the challenge to be totally free. art can be a part of this challenge, a part of the adventure, & yet we use art as a shelter, or we stifle the creative process with fear & worry and manipulate our work so that it becomes a safe & respectable thing to do. art has been divided from life and we shld attempt to end this division, it is a division which denies art and life. within all of this is the idea that the self is not the center of art; but only by seeing the self clearly can we be free of it, however momentarily, & not thru any amnt of suppression or repression, or so-called meditation. increasingly l am interested in working cooperatively & the traditional ways of being an artist, writing a bk or having a solo show or wotever, really dont hold too much relevance or interest. in our "garden nerns" show at powerhouse gallery pat walsh & l workt cooperatively (as cold mountain productions) mixing & pouring 7,000 lbs of concrete, pouring it into holes dug in the earth, & then moving it to the gallery. we neednt work in isolation when it is possible to join other people in free expression & cooperation. but this can only be done if one is vulnerable & allows the insecurity of life & art to be realized, which partly means seeing that the self with its preconceptions abt wot is art & wot is not art has nothing to do with the work except as a point of departure into the work.

2.

any movement to create an individual style eventually presupposes saying things in a certain preconceived way, having a definite way of seeing reality. style is the self in another form, the self demanding continuity in words and ideas and, eventually subordinating saying anything new to a whole array of ideas & opinions abt who I am & wot I believe, cutting off any perception of the new with presuppositions and the safety of the old. style that becomes consistency in writing becomes conformity to the past; while in fact each piece shld be new, we shld move thru a cluster of styles; style as a transitory event, not as a conclusion which manipulates reality to agree with how one writes. either one moves with the demands of reality or one's work atrophies. if we work according to formulas and rules art eventually gives way to shadows and darkness, to an area of the mind which seeks security in the old and finds only the dulling repetition of the past & the self.

3.

Krishnamurti writes that art is skill in action & differentiates between expression & self expression. a clever mind, a mind cultivated with knowledge and experience, can turn out a reasonable poem, but to investigate something without the center, the center which says there is a right way & a wrong way to see things, that investigation is an art, whether poetry or the art of listening, listening without the center, without thot. or to write a poem which is an expression of a certain quality of the mind, a quality of austerity & humility, of not knowing, of insecurity, which isnt being aware from a position; the expression of this quality of the mind which is sensitive to reality seems to me to be essential to art and life, & not merely the repetition of the past or remaining within the security of ideas and beliefs, where the mind can move only within the field of the known and the dead.

4.

one of the biggest errors is to separate the arts, or to claim someone is more of a visual artist than someone else becuz they have been at it longer. as soon as we bring time into art we are back into the games of society. becuz psychologically freedom is a perception which has nothing to do with time. and unless art is a perception, that is, a moment of free expression, of passive awareness & insight, then we are back into someone being more of an artist than someone else becuz they have been at it longer. art has nothing to do with time. you do it & if it's a "good" piece or not doesnt depend on how many pieces you've done before but on the quality of perception which creates it. as soon as we bring time into art we set up grades and divisions, who is superior and who is inferior. skill to hold a brush or to write a coherent sentence requires chronological time, clock time; seeing things clearly, freedom of perception, psychological freedom, has nothing to do with time or the movement of time as thought. it seems to me that art lies in this perception which radically changes all aspects of one's life.

5.

real art lies in the insecurity of life. as long as we live or create by formulas or promote some ideology or point of view, a set of beliefs or opinions from which we interpret, analyze or speculate abt life, then we continue the past in a modified form. the only creation there is lies in a perception from insecurity, security based on the accumulation of thot, of the past, creates nothing but contradiction and narrows both life and perception. everyday is a new creation but we attempt to meet its challenge with the old. the old brought into the present creates nothing but unhappiness and conflict. the very joy & freedom of art & life is the hidden presence of insecurity.

Garden Nerns by Stephen Morrissey and Pat Walsh, 1977.

THE GLORY OF A GREAT PAST

—John McAuley

Concrete Poetry: The Story of a Further Journey

John McAuley

Montreal Journal of Poetics 1:1, Winter 1978-79

The pictorial foundation of writing can be substantiated by many more anecdotes than I can tell here, but I will relate two which validate this cultural response. In the late 18th century an Englishman was shipwrecked and cast ashore in the Tonga Islands, a kind of paradise. There a white man had never been seen before, and was considered by the native inhabitants as a ghost returned to the land of the living. He began to write a narrative using a solution of glue and gunpowder. The King became very interested in the "ghost's" activities and commanded that his name be put down in the mystic signs. When the sailor did this the Royal Name was read aloud. The King was greatly bewildered as he gazed at the script which the "ghost" had scribbled. The King frowned and said, "This is not me, where are my legs?" Further afield, from an earlier period, Chinese tradition ascribes the invention of writing to the dragon-faced, four-eyed sage Ts'ang Chien who saw in the stars of heaven the footprints of birds and the marks on the back of a tortoise, the models for his invention of written characters.

These two versions of the pictorial origin of writing also make known to us the power writing once held, a power of enchantment which has been encircled by and immersed in a sea of print in this Word Age. Now, the concrete poem is a transmutation "subito pianissimo" of the *pictura* that is speech, expressed in primitive though exalted glyphs. The concrete poem still retains the ancient power of picture writing because it shows, rather than tells, the way a tarot card centers reality.

It seems quite possible that picture writing, concrete poetry and tarot are continually created in the face of a hidden knowledge once truly serviceable to man. This can be inferred by one outstanding actuality: the library of Rameses II at Thebes bore the inscription "The Hospital of the Soul" over its entrance. But this hidden knowledge was lost, at a later date, in the destruction of the great library at Alexandria in Egypt where a million zephyrous and fragile manuscripts had been centralized from all over the ancient world. The secrets of reality those manuscripts contained we would call occult. It is said they documented the scenery and allurements of the "Great Time" before the over-civilizing of man.

While tarot has remained in the occult camp and picture writing in the hands of isolated tribal shamans, only concrete poetry (an offshoot of both) interests the contemporary wordsmith because it offers the observant poet an opportunity to work with the *occultation* of experience on *his* terms. For the pictura, concrete poem and tarot, form becomes a limitless source of content beyond the "forbidden lines" where narrative expression fails to reduplicate the pattern of its intensive parable, its beginning, middle, its moral logic and end. Concrete poetry penetrates words letting space confide its secrets without the slavery of comparison that words can sometimes cause in their urgency to be understood. Consequently, concrete poetry suffers no convenient imposition of rhetoric and maps instead the all clear region of intuition where consciousness and the unconscious meet. A concrete poem is simply a decorative score composed of two salients, with any distinguished continuum known as a "head band" and any fading area called a "tail band."

The beguiling simplicity of a concrete poem should not mislead us into the assumption that it represents mere typographical fiddling. We must remember its origins in the hidden knowledge of ages past. It preserves a persistent connotation that names are integral parts of images and objects, though the modern alphabet of Phoenician invention to expedite trade and commerce has almost lost this attribution. Yet today, concrete poetry continues to revitalize older embodiments of hidden power, transforming the consonant *M* for example, into a nocturnal owl or altering other letters such as *A* from its status as vowel and article into the soaring diurnal eagle, all partners in an endless passage.

—Tom Konyves

Newspapers and Open Field Poetry

John McAuley

The Insecurity of Art, 1982

It isn't far from the truth to say that a poem is shaped or designed with the influence of the newspaper lurking at the back of the maker's mind. In a single morning *The Montreal Gazette* sells more copies in this city than does all the new poetry published across Canada from New Year's Day to Christmas. In one year the people of Montreal read a mind boggling number of newspapers, which if collected and stacked by the Fire Department would create a tower casting a shadow at daybreak from Mount Royal to Los Angeles; a shadow that by noon would cross the icy crest of the North Pole. Time devoted to this wanton consumption of news, symbolized by an albeit improbable sweeping shadow so vast that the continent itself becomes a sundial, shows the scope of people's psychic need for newspapers to interpret and clarify the world and their place in it. Reading newspapers is a popular ritual—as pervasive as brushing teeth. The daily consumption of newspapers indicates the population is hooked on a gargantuan habit. Newspaper strikes are especially hard for people to bear. When denied a major newspaper, they will turn to supermarket tabloids and drugstore scandal sheets just as dope addicts smoke seeds and hash pipe scrapings to avoid going cold turkey. Clearly, newspapers provide a cosmic "rush" in print. If poetry ever had this kind of effect on a population maybe Homer and Virgil knew something about it, but those days are gone. Newspapers have stolen poetry's circulation by casting everyday legends. It appears the public appetite for news has increased exponentially. This is a fair assumption considering unlike the classical notion that heroes were to last as long as white marble, a contemporary saviour like Jim Jones becomes a devil overnight having instigated a grape Koolaid crusade into the Hereafter. Public attention may be brief but it is demanding, the public is fascinated by death. Sacrifice seems larger and more real than life.

Perfect for saviours and heroes is the newspaper's inverted pyramid style. Its mode is to present the most important fact first, followed by a train of lesser facts. The problem with the inverted pyramid style is that it defies gravity, the pull and tug of reality, causing facts to float in a romantic cloud of history. But why should interpretation of events be subordinated to a set formula or method? Newspapers outlive their founding editors and generations of journalists: all believers in an impersonal journalese. Traditionally, they are members of the Fourth Estate fulfilling the dynamic function of giving the public what it wants, a vicarious high of tragedy, crises and comedy in a patchwork of sheets taken from wire services around the world. Newspapers print for the public good, hence journalists collaborate with society rather than with life. The fatal error of the romantic journalist is that he, like the misguided evangelist, imagines himself to be a measurer of life and finds truth in a hierarchy of facts, the latter in paranoid revelations. Today, poets are practicing an unheard, unread craft, writing persistently as the last repositories of individual conscience fashioning, in the words of Frank O'Hara, "visual biographical emblems." The poet doesn't glorify the plight of an individual in the manner of a journalist, the poet explores and experiences an event and its consequences simultaneously as he creates, travelling the pathway of art which Geoffrey of Vinsauf wrote about eight centuries ago in "Poetria Nova." The poem follows a loose and adaptable periodic pathway and reveals first what was later in time and defers the appearance of what was actually earliest. The poem's path leads to the discovery of a pyramid, apex up, firmly grounded in the sands of life. The periodic structure of poetry is life's imprint in the affirmative language of our hearts and minds, our emotions and desires.

Many years ago a Frenchman, Stephane Mallarmé considered the subtle psychological influence of newspapers in an inscrutable observation:

> It is a virgin space, face to face
> with the lucidity of our matching vision
> divided of itself in solitude, into halves
> of whiteness; and each of these is lawful
> bride at the wedding of the idea.

What Mallarmé was getting at is that the page of a newspaper is a collage-like mosaic of varying typefaces, designed for the eye like Greek temples. Fortunately for poetry, Mallarmé's discovery of the page as a habitus for words remained attractive for others. The Imagists and succeeding poets like Charles Olson all took Mallarmé's brides to ceremonial vows proclaiming an old Arabian proverb: "The eye sleeps until the mind wakes it with a question." The marriage of the newspaper mosaic with the periodic design of the poem has become known as Open Field Poetry. This cohabitation is based on the virtues of form as the key to life. Words in a periodic mosaic express parenthesis without subordination. Words become democratized in a way Whitman never dreamed of.

While the newspaper mosaic locks language into the linear and vertical grid of a chronicle of facts it remains a superficial historical tableau. The poetic mosaic depicts a gathering of voices in isolation, a harmony of self-ironic images and a composition of metaphors crafted by an intelligence spanning nothing more than the poles between inner and outer worlds of possibility. The poet's concern with individuality and subsequent search for individuality in the form offered by Open Field Poetry has given the art its first advance in "amplification" (the technique of expansion) since the codification of tropes and figures in Classical times. A quotation from 'The Descent' by William Carlos Williams will, I trust, clarify the thrust of this explication.

> No defeat is made up entirely of defeat—since
> the world it opens is always a place
> formerly
> unsuspected. A
> world lost,
> a world unsuspected,
> and no whiteness (lost) is so white as the memory
> of whiteness.

—John McAuley

Drummer Boy Raga: Red Light, Green Light

John Mc Auley Ken Norris Tom Konyves Andre Farkas
Opal L. Nations Stephen Morrissey (R.pert)

and others

Sat.Apr.16, 1977 8:00 P.M.

3738 St-Dominique **844-3489**

Powerhouse Gallery

Videopoetry

Tom Konyves

Montreal Journal of Poetics 1:1, Winter 1978-79

I have come to gradually surrender my poetic power to a medium which devours words much like fire devours paper.

Screening tapes made earlier at a reading, I became aware of a certain "power" which actually transformed the poet to performer then attempted to "putrefy" the experience into a neatly-framed (silent as the ages) fossil.

The lack of a cohesive poetic experience on the screen not only created doubts about my own poems but forced the resolution to discover why certain things "worked" while others did not.

I screened 15 hours of poetry before putting together the hour-and-a-half production "Poetry On Tape" (1977) which included Steve McCaffery, Anne Waldman, Stephen Morrissey and Pat Walsh, and "Drummer Boy Raga: Red Light, Green Light," a six-poet "collaboration." By the time I began recording readings myself, I had an inkling of what I was looking for.

Screening, in the terminology of video production, is the ritual one succumbs to like the repeated chants in the Koran—simplistic repetition. (We all know the value of repetition as a purgative and proof of faith.) Two immediate observations: the poet on the screen was less effective than 'real life' and the camera could (a) refuse to participate, (b) choose to collaborate and even (c) dominate. Video had the propensity to render poetry as recital, extremely static. The best became revealed as sudden bursts of energy. An hour-reel was yielding about five minutes of sustained energy.

The printed word was looking more and more like a secret message sent from room to room, from the poet's den to the reader's bedchamber. In other words, a certain immediacy was lacking. Readings attempt to restore a missing link—the voice—while audio and video recordings wish to create a new immediacy, albeit an artificial one.

The printed poem faces no great obstacle as audio and video-poems do. Radio and television have no offshoot comparable to the small press which actually "sells" poetry in limited but consistent quantities to an audience who appreciates pale covers and neat stanzas, delighting in well-groomed dogs and math textbooks.

Taped recordings and records (discs) of poetry, although few, are dedicated to preserving "classics" first and foremost. Experimental works comprise a very small portion of available tapes and records. Their contribution to the craft has been, to be fair, infinitesimal. The past twenty-five years have attempted to restore sound to words but the results seemed to confirm the role of print as the "natural" medium rather than what English profs declare perfunctorily to their students: poetry was oral in its state of innocence. Poetry has become so that, as art proper, the book has become the indwelling of its soul.

But the hare of technology never sleeps, he's just recharging his batteries. Radio and television believe in poetry only as far as the next ad. Poetry is rejected as viable programming mainly because of the market in its "own" field: if poetry books don't sell, poetry doesn't sell.

It is alarming that there is a little bit of poetry in everything but by no means is there a little bit of everything in poetry. The state of the art is in crisis.

When your own medium rejects you (newspapers used to publish a poem a day), like any business, you change or die. Poemists have sanctified the "personal revelatory" nature of poetry and consigned it to "book" forms. For books will always be there...

Poetry has been more than welcome in theatre (Beckett), music (Dylan), film (Cocteau), and visual art (Johns)...

Children hear before they see, hear words before they see words and see words before they spell words (badly). And reading permits rereading, which distorts the true unfolding of the poem.

Tape sheds the binding cords of decipher-by-participation, turn-back-the-page-before-continuing poetry experience one becomes accustomed to. (A New York poetess distributed mimeographed copies of her poems before her reading. Reading them (with her) gave me the feeling of pissing in the sea. Listening to her wasn't that great, either.)

Writing for video should be easy enough. It is more malleable than print or audio-tape. A good poem on tape will use all technology has to offer, repetition, dubbing, music mix, unexpected periods of silence, untranslatable sounds. "Special effects" will be the vocabulary of this new poem.

"It's interesting, but it's just not poetry." Yet the tape-recorded poem is as far advanced now as printing was when poems were handwritten. Print is by no means at an end. But its usefulness, in our sphere, is diminishing.

What then of print?

The role of print should be the scoring of a performance. The poem, as we know it, is the monologue of a poetry theatre.

Collaboration is increasing, but monologues abound. In print, mind you, not video. Access is easy enough, technical know-how takes time and patience, but after that the medium is limitless.

Some "monologues" are so fascinating that many poets never transcend "recitals." But the one-voice-theory is a limitation today's poets must beware of. In a poetry theatre, what we know as the poem serves two purposes—sings a plaint to divert the audience or paints a scene or object. Video allows poets to see their roles more clearly, and it is to this end I strive. Whereas I consider a line the unit of poem-making, like bricklaying, in video we substitute visual lines for printed lines and proceed to "layer" a poem: spoken words (the poet-performer); words heard (taped, dubbed); and seen (signs, subtitles, printed, painted). Naturally, a poem written with these three forms of wordsmithing is never "itself" until it is meshed with visual imagery (close-ups, cuts, dissolves, pans). If the end-product demonstrates a "judicious" mix of the two (even an interesting interplay) the poem will have a texture we will all admire.

Bad video is as possible as bad poetry. A poetry theatre attempts to take a stance somewhere between the documentation of a poem and creating a poem of dialogue, music and visual effects. The poetry, the words, should be the real motion of the piece. The other media will support and collaborate to this end. When language is "raised to poetry" other media ultimately give way to this language.

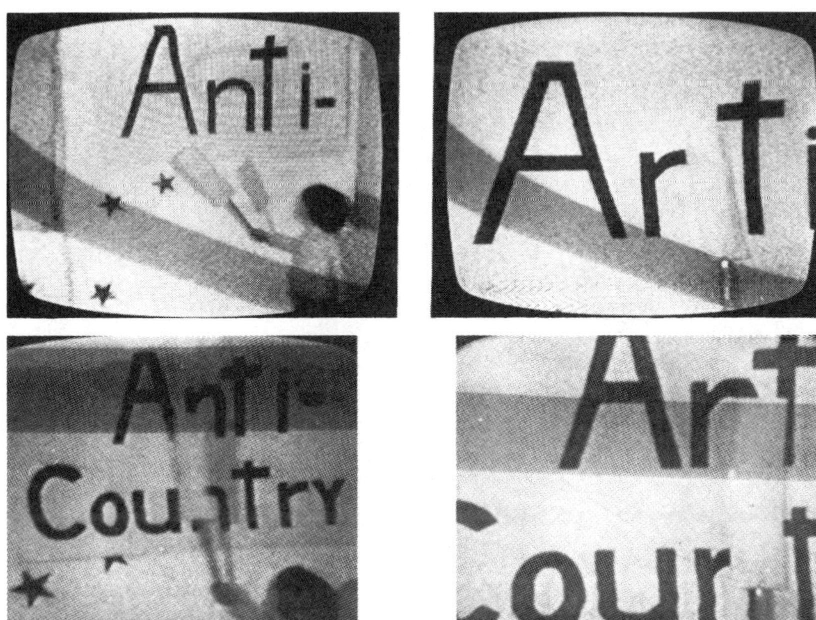

—from "See/Saw,"1977.

"Face Off." Standing (left to right): Gurney Bolster, Carol Harwood, Michel Bonneau, Evelyn Ginzburg, Howard Abrams. Sitting: Sylvie St. Laurent. 1980.

"Close Up" at The Music Gallery in Toronto. Endre Farkas and Keith Daniel. 1979.

Confessions of a Collaborator

Endre Farkas

Montreal Journal of Poetics, 1978-80

1.

We are all collaborators. We can't help it. We just aren't always aware of it. Art seems to be the exception and poetry and poets have created a dark romantic mystique about being solitary creators. On the surface, it certainly seems to be true. But beneath that mystique, a lot of "collaborative" work is going on.

In poetry, the initial collaboration is between the poet and the muse. The degree of collaboration varies from poet to poet as well as from poem to poem. There is no formula. It is conscious, unconscious, seductive, brutal, mundane and/or ritualistic. Collaboration with the muse (call it what you will) is one that takes you out of this world, puts you outside of the "norm" where the collaboration defines where and what you are. It is what makes for a lone-wolf existence even if one is in a relationship. It creates the world that becomes the poem and that poem is what leads you back to the daily. The poem is the postcard the poet and the muse send back ending with "wish you were here."

At one time or another, as readers, we have collaborated in making the poem live. By the physical act of picking up a book of poems, opening it and reading, we work with the poet. In a very real sense, we make the poem(s) kinetic. We breathe our life into a poem which, until then, existed in a potential state. And, of course, if the poem is true, it breathes its life into us.

Then there is the poet/poem/reader collaboration. The first time I became conscious of this poet/poem/reader collaboration process was when I read the collaborative poem "Pull My Daisy" by Ginsberg, Kerouac & Cassidy. The poem and especially the idea of collaboration excited me. I got off on the idea that poets, usually loners, got together to make a poem. Also, the "making" of a poem by three poets struck me as a radical, anti-poetical act. I got off on that too! Here were three individuals, of sympathetic sensibilities, be-bopping, scatting and filling out an auditory space with crazy line & image exchanges. The poem is woven by a poet called G.K.C. When I read it out loud, I heard a collective chant of serious play.

However, it was only a year or so later that I participated in my first collaborative poem. It was with John McAuley, an experimental sound, concrete poet. I was living on a commune (a cosmic omen?) and John came up for a few days. One evening we started to tape a letter he wanted to send to bpNichol and ended up with a sense-sound collage. We were involved in serious play and I experienced the same kind of rush as on first reading "Pull My Daisy."

I must admit that, at first, because of my academic conditioning, this play made me feel guilty. To be having fun making poems, an art which my teachers wrote, taught, analyzed & expected dry essays on—and making it collaboratively to boot—seemed sacrilegious. But John, who was more familiar and at ease with it teased me over the fence of guilt into the garden of delights. He made me aware of the possibilities of the solitary & collaborative letting go process. Thanks Long John.

Collaborations, at first, were not something I planned in advance; rather, they tended to be spontaneous both in the choice of collaborators and the idea for collaboration. My first (still in existence) collaborative poem was with a stranger whom, even now, I only know as Mash. He was just passing through in the summer of 73 and heard of an open reading at Véhicule and stopped by to recite some of his poems. I liked them and we ended up going out for some beers, having an all night rap, reading to each other (our own & favourites) and parted with a vague promise to keep in touch.

A couple of months later I got a letter from him and in it were four lines of what was to become our collaborative poem. I added to it & sent it back. This went on for a couple of months with lines, words & syntax being changed, interrupted, reconstructed and deleted until I lost track of him somewhere in South America. The poem is a collage of his 'on the road' experience & my fixedness. There is a weave of the two experiences and the sense of one voice filling the road & home. This voice was neither mine nor his but a third that was the result of our union. An inner & outer sacred geography was being travelled, mapped and moved on from.

2.

My next collaboration, "Er/Words/Ah/Bridge," was a result of events & attitudes rather than another poet. It is a piece that was triggered by a George Bowering reading & a flute & koto concert.

Bowering read mainly from *Autobiology* and I was struck by the flow that was created by the modulation of phrases & images. The narrative moved (maybe wove is a better verb) on these recurring phrases, spiraling from sense to nonsense to innocence. The piece created its impact & meaning via the resonances & phrase couplings. He used Stein-like structures to organically connect his listeners/readers to the processes of growth.

A week later I attended a flute & koto concert at McGill. Between each piece the Caucasian flautist would elaborate on Oriental compositional traditions. However, because of his irritating (at first) habit of stringing "er/ah" bridge sounds throughout his explanation I could not follow his stories. The "er/ahs" increased until phrases & words became islands in a sea of "er/ahs." And as islands they became meaningless in the linear sense and I began to concentrate on the bridge sounds. I found that the bridge sounds expressed eloquently the inexpressible beauty of the music that was being performed.

These two events were the catalyst for something. I knew that much, but where I was going to go with this "something" I had no idea. I knew that I wanted to do something with those "er/ahs" and I knew that I didn't want to describe my feelings about the music & the reading and that the piece could not be in any traditional form. The above conclusions were more felt than logically deduced. It was this intuitive leap and a sense of play that led me to the "how" making of this piece. "Er/Words/Ah/ Bridge" is a poem integrating various elements of chance. I used the width of the 8.5 x 11 sheet to determine the length of the line (16 words). I cut up the Entertainment section of *The Montreal Star* and mixed the pieces up in an envelope. The first stanza, beginning with "Er," has a sequentially increasing number of "ers" (alternating with words) until all 16 "words" are "ers."

The second stanza introduces the "ahs" in reverse until all the "'ers" are pushed back & off the page. This makes the second stanza a visual as well as a pure sound stanza.

The third stanza is a combination of "ah"s & words with the words appearing from the right hand side & combining in a fashion similar to the first stanza.

This poem was the first that I *made*. I was responding in kind to the reading & concert. I found the making interesting because the execution was so definitely tied to time & form. Most of the time a poem happens and with it the form, minus revision, but that was not the case here. I felt that I was involved more in the plastic arts and in fact did follow up with a visual collage of "Er/Words/Ah/Bridge."

The poem has also had an interesting reading history. I first read it as a poem for one voice; fairly straightforward. It was a piece that demanded a lot from both reader & listener. It was definitely a performance piece. As a one-voice piece I found myself putting emphasis on the words to create an absurd linear text and using the bridge sounds as a form of chorus. There were limitations in one voice as well as harsh wear & tear on the vocal chords. Perhaps I could get past some of the limitations now that I've had more performance experience with "sound," but then, those two reasons were enough to seek out another voice. I asked Carol Harwood to perform it with me and the two-voice combinations (plus the male-female pitches) produced a more diverse effect.

Since two voices worked & there were three stanzas...why not? Ken Norris has been that third voice and with the establishment of this trio, we have started to evolve this piece where now even the words have been broken down to sounds, have been recombined with the "er/ahs" and words & sounds stretched & layered so that a tactile auditory experience is created and is being evolved with each performance.

I have gone into such detail of the making of this piece because, for me, it contained experimental elements that I had not previously explored. I knew of, had seen & heard concrete & sound poetry, but had not really attempted to work with the forms. And until the making of this piece, that is all that they were—forms. But then I realized that the same intense passions came into play. Also this piece made public my interest & concerns for experimental poetry which, I'm 20/20 hindsight sure, pointed the way to & connected me with other poets who were also working to make it new. In Montreal these poets were also "community minded," involved in organizing readings, magazines & presses and collaborations.

3.

"Drummer Boy Raga: Red Light/Green Light" was the next collaboration I got involved with. Tom Konyves was the instigator. He asked John McAuley, Stephen Morrissey, Opal L. Nations, Ken Norris & me to collaborate.

I said yes, but like so often, I said yes before really seeing what it was going to entail. However, I think that there are times when this "take a chance" attitude is necessary both in writing and living. To be quite honest, I must admit that for a while I didn't really know what Tom's intent was aside from doing it.

The text was a concept—a chain letter-manuscript which upon receiving you manipulated, collaged or added to and sent it on to the next person for his version of the process. My contribution was an already existing piece, a list poem "Exercise for Body/ Mind/ Soul." I cut it up and inserted the lines at random. The chain mail collaboration went on for a couple of months and included a couple of rehearsals. The overall effect was not one of cohesion. I don't think it was meant to be. The performance was forgettable because 1) there were too many of us (nine including a drummer, flautist and dancer), and 2) it was too linear. It was the fact of coming together rather than the performance that stands out in my mind. It was also the first time I got a sense of community in this city. You don' t know what community is until you've got it; it isn't everybody being buddy-buddy & kissing each other's work. It is more the challenge of allowing everyone to take their own chances as well as coming together to learn.

This was also the first time I got a glimpse of Tom's organizational and creative process. He reminded me of a spiffed-up, mad cook concocting surreal urban dishes, chopping them up in city-order with dashes of silence. Even then he was feeling his way to those spaces where "words can never say."

4.

For about five years, I was involved with contemporary dancers, composers and actors in collaborations that had me writing in a way I never thought of as a poet. I wrote "texts" not poems. Texts that had a narrative sense but not a linear one. I wrote them as the performance piece was evolving, to suit a move or create a mood to which moves could be choreographed or improvised. I also danced and partook in the performances. As I rehearsed, I became aware of breath pacing: fast, slow, normal, breathless, etc. Working with dancers taught me how to listen to the breath. The texts tended to be minimal and repetitive: modular, until the minimal repetitiveness filled the space and enveloped the audience. I really liked working with the dancers because I felt that I was making the poem kinetic in a new and exciting way. Over a period of 5 years, I collaborated on 5 dance/performance pieces.

Working with a composer was more problematic because it was *his* concept, although I was intrigued and challenged by working in a discipline in which I had always been told I was inept. In school I was constantly told I was unmusical. I am tone deaf but writing had made me feel that I certainly was sensitive to rhythm (in poetry anyway). So working with a composer on a "sound piece" seemed like a wonderful way into the world of music. However, this collaboration had more conflict than collaboration. He really didn't have much interest in my contribution other than as another sound source and I resented it. I also found his ideas too conceptual and dry. He wanted to wire me for sound: he wanted electrodes and microphones attached to various parts of my body: head, nose, throat, arms, chest and back. Then he wanted me to read my piece while wired to a computer that would make random selections of sound source(s) to amplify. So the text would be interrupted at the whim of a machine. The text in this collaboration was engaged in a battle for survival against becoming just sound. I guess I didn't want to admit that the poem (the words) was just another sound. So I began "Call me

Interface..." and ended with a fielder (baseball) making a grab for the final out. It was a collage of something borrowed, something new, something modular and something else. The reason I can't quote it is that after the final performance at 4 o'clock in the morning (which went badly) I left the text (the only copy) behind. But even though I resented the idea of a poem becoming just sound, my awareness of the sound aspect of poems was heightened and I guess that's why I didn't quit. This piece was performed across Canada.

Collaborating with dancers and performing contributed to my awareness of being a performer and of my relation to space, time and audience. This was further enhanced when I began to work on *An Evening in the Muses' Company*. I imagined the concept to be a performance/ cabaret evening that would showcase the various performance pieces I had developed and were to conceive for the evening. I realized that although I liked collaborating, I liked being in charge. The collaborations were more rewarding when I had originated the concept and had an outline which could be elaborated by the other collaborators. I chose to work with Michel Bonneau and Genevieve Raymond, friends who had backgrounds in theatre, dance and music. They were quite supportive of the process. It was the most pleasant collaborative process of all. Each one of us found our niche. I would write text, Michel and Genevieve would respond not only to the text but to how it would translate to stage. What I learned from this collaboration is the importance of silence, how a gesture or a look could convey pages of text. I learned to eliminate excessive description. I also learned to feel for a text and saw how the same text and actions could evolve night after night. I learned how to listen and because of that how to write.

Collaboration, for me, was a need to balance the isolation I felt as a writer. It also let me see how other artists from other disciplines worked and it made me realize that art without a community benefits no one and serves no purpose.

5. Epilogue

I wound down my "public" collaborations around 1983 when my daughter was born. All-night rehearsals and discussions gave way to midnight feedings, diaper changes and early risings. My collaboration with the word/poem returned to the page, not only as poet, but as publisher. I began to publish other people's work on a regular basis. My approach to publishing is collaborative rather than hierarchical. I do select the manuscripts, but the authors are often intimately involved in the production and design of their books. This collaborative work is still going on and it has its own pleasure and pain.

The New World

Ken Norris

Montreal Journal of Poetics 1:2, Spring-Summer 1979

In 1943, in his introduction to the *Book of Canadian Poetry*, A.J.M. Smith was able to discern two "schools" or orientations in Canadian poetry, the "cosmopolitan" and the "native":

> Canadian poetry, indeed, is the record of life in Canada as it takes on significance when all the resources of sensibility, intelligence, and spirit are employed in experiencing it or in understanding it. Some of the poets have concentrated on what is individual and unique in Canadian life and others upon what it has in common with life everywhere. The one group has attempted to describe and interpret whatever is essentially and distinctively Canadian and thus come to terms with an environment that is only now ceasing to be colonial. The other, from the very beginning, has made a heroic effort to transcend colonialism by entering into the universal, civilizing culture of ideas.

Those writers who concentrated on what is "individual and unique in Canadian life" Smith considered to be the "natives"; the "cosmopolitans" (a group that Smith clearly feels more of an affinity with), on the other hand, have "made a heroic effort to transcend colonialism by entering the universal, civilizing culture of ideas." In essence, the cosmopolitans have imported a culture and idea of civilization that originated with English and European forebears, whereas the colonial natives have tried to work with what they found upon encountering the reality of *this* continent.

There has always been something incredibly false about trying to turn the Americas into some mirror image of Europe & it is a process that has continually failed since the beginning. Blake's vision of America did not materialize simply because the continent itself demanded to have its say. You can try to dump the diverse cultures into a melting pot or organize them into a mosaic but there is still that something which the Aztecs and other Indians knew of and sacrificed to that haunts this expanse of land, and which transforms everything it touches, making it native. Susanna Moodie could tenaciously cling to the ways of the English gentlewoman as she struggled with her family to survive in the bush, but she is most beautiful and most real when she stops fighting against the land that she is standing on and everything that surrounds her and undergoes those small instances of transformation when she becomes a living creature sensitized to where she is and what the place and instant demand.

To A.J.M. Smith in 1943 one of the greatest crimes for an author was to be colonial, this assessment coming in the wake of the jingoistic navel-gazings of the Canadian Authors' Association and the endless prattlings of the likes of Sir Charles G.D. Roberts and Bliss Carman, two nature poets who didn't have a clue as to where they really were. Smith was asserting that a poet couldn't go through the world with blinders on while the petulant muse dangled a maple leaf before his nose. He was right, Canada *did* have to be pried open in order to let modernism in. But he was also wrong in rejecting the sense of place for a dream of cultured drawing-rooms: by doing this he greatly limited himself by adopting established poetic forms and embracing fully the English poetic tradition. He severed all ties with the land and became a Europeanized Canadian academic poet teaching in an American university. His compatriot, Frank Scott, although also willing to adopt English forms at times, did not turn away from what the land presented, from what was *there*; instead he carved out timeless poems such as "Old Song" and "Laurentian Shield" which stand as testimonies, not to Canada, but to the territories Canada inhabits, the land that lies under the feet of a conceptual nation.

When Charles Olson spoke of the SPACE of America and the idea of locale he was only echoing what William Carlos Williams and D.H. Lawrence had begun to say in their books *In the American Grain* and *Studies in Classic American Literature* in the 1920's. What Williams and Lawrence couldn't get over was the nature of the places; the land shouted so loudly to them it could almost drown out the steel mills of the east coast. And Williams couldn't get over how much the entire American society had tried to avoid the reality of the land, save for the sole saint in Williams' American cosmology: Daniel Boone. Boone got to know the land, the Indians, entered into a harmonic relationship with the wilderness rather than taking part in the Puritan steamrolling that eventually asphalted and paved the United States from coast to coast. While the thirteen colonies were following the words of wisdom and prosperity set down in Franklin's *Poor Richard's Almanack* Boone was out in the hills, getting to know the wildlife and fauna, rubbing his body with the rich dark earth.

There is something about this continent that refutes Smith's wanting poetry to deal with what life here "has in common with life everywhere," and this refutation is voiced in Charles Olson's essay "Human Universe":

> It is not the Greeks I blame. What it comes to is ourselves, that we do not find ways to hew to experience as it is, in our definition and expression of it, and not be led to partition reality at any point, in any way. For this is just what we do, this is the real issue of what has been, and the process, as it now asserts itself, can be exposed. It

> is the function, *comparison*, or, its bigger name, *symbology*. These are the false faces, too much seen, which hide and keep from us the active intellectual states, metaphor and performance. All that comparison ever does is set up a series of reference points: to compare is to take one thing and try to understand it by marking its similarities to or difference from another. Right here is the trouble, that each thing is not so much like or different from another thing (these likenesses and differences are apparent) but that such an analysis only accomplishes a *description*, does not come to grips with what really matters: that a thing, any thing, impinges on us by a more important fact, its self-existence, without reference to any other thing, in short, the very character of it calls our attention to it, which wants us to know more about it, its particularity. This is what we are confronted by, not the thing's "class," any hierarchy, of quality or quantity, but the thing itself, and its *relevance* to ourselves who are the experience of it (whatever it may mean to someone else, or whatever other relations it may have).

If Black Mountain poetics make sense to Canadian poets it's only because the natural philosophies of it make so much sense: the demand for particularity, the writing of where you are, the necessity for understanding your own breathing and your own articulation: and ultimately it goes back to Williams crying out in the name of the wilderness, shouting at the top of his gentle lungs: "We're *here*, you silly buggers! *Here*! Pay attention! Forget about abstract Beauty and look at that deer in the brush! Listen to that bird call and forget about the music of the spheres!" For Williams knew that we *are* in a new world, live on the face of a continent that is not young but has an ancient consciousness over which we've spread our inherited European sophistications like a table cloth. What matters most are the things that are unique to this place, this life experience—the buffalo and the hummingbirds—not the polyglot rehashings of transplanted Prousts. We don't need that. The commonality of all life is best reflected in the individual ways in which life manifests itself, and there is much of the specific nature of this continent that we haven't even started to write about.

PROVERBSI #42

TV is Christ.

Tom Konyves and Ken Norris (with plaster cast of John McAuley) at Véhicule Art Gallery, 1978.

Claudia Lapp reading at Véhicule Art Gallery, 1972.

Some Aspects of Dreams & Poetry

Claudia Lapp

Montreal Journal of Poetics 1:3, Spring-Summer 1980

I watch the frozen lake
and its surface begins to buckle
and the water comes into motion

who knows how long I've been standing here
as the motion of another season begins
and luminous wave patterns fill my winter eyes

Fragment from a longer dream-movie, image which also represents an aspect of my life in time. Written as the above "poem" spontaneously, no changes made. Lifted out of the dream context, what meaning does it have for me, for others who read it or listen to it? Meaning for me, since lifting it from the dream-weave makes it more salient to me (in dream it was just a few frames in a longer movie full of many telescoped messages from the unconscious). But does this personal psychic energy packet contain *de quoi* for others? We can't say it's archetypal, but it is about solid becoming fluid, winter transitting into warmth, and the wave patterns, they can become whatever the listener has in mind. So this dream image goes beyond the personal dream dimension. And in the years I've been writing dream poetry, I have preserved only those that were wide enough for sharing.

We've been hoarding dreams too long (although some of Kerouac's in his *Book of Dreams*, he *should* have held onto!), and I have a calling to preserve dream info energy beauty by voicing it for the community, whatever scope that circle has—friend or two, family, and outward. The Senoi, a Malaysian tribe who've gotten much attention in the alternative culture media, when studied in the 30s, used dreams to take care of the personal/collective psychic demons and thus maintained a pretty undiseased state: "The Senoi say that dreams of sexual love should always move through orgasm, and the dreamer should always demand from his dream lover the poem, the song, the dance, the useful knowledge which will express the beauty of his/her spiritual lover to the group..." [1]

What a native Australian once said is no longer quite true, that:

White man got no dreamin'
Him go 'nother way
White man, him go different.

One of my reasons in persisting to record dreams and translate them into a poem form is because I know they are parts of a natural healing and repair process which is both individual (as when you're told that your pipes are clogged) and collective (images of future group work and service).

Poetry that proceeds from dreams? Let me give some personal history:

on a black horse
with moon-shaped hooves
blowing a green glass trumpet
he came
on the tide of dream debris...

When I awoke the feeling was so tangible, the image so real I had no choice but to record what I'd just seen indream. I was charged with the energy of the image. This was a clear message from a deep image-making source. I call it neptunian (the sea, the horse—one of Poseidon's forms, the green glass conch). OK. Animus figure. OK. Recalling Stephan Crane's "Black Riders," which I encountered four years later (Neptune is prophetic):

Black riders came from the sea.
There was clang and clang of spear and shield...
Wild shouts and wave of hair
in rush upon the wind:
Thus the ride of Sin. [2]

"On a Black Horse," coming from the multi-dimensioned dreamspace, can't be reduced to a single level meaning. It continues to generate significance seven years later; it changes as I change. People like it for various reasons. It evokes freedom, death, mystery of eros, dissolution of past. Not to suggest that only dream writing has this quality, but to recall the pleasure of receiving a clear image on the inner screen so effortlessly.

Three years ago I received a dream with the pristine quality that marks a "big" dream. It dealt with feminine concerns of being caged in, mutilated, of ritual group cleansing and application of make-up to conceal blood. We women were represented by a tiny wounded forest animal. There were men outside our powder-room-in-the-woods-retreat. They were wearing red and were threatening, until we faced them, made peace with them, and could continue on our forest journey together. There followed many dreams of working on a big Opus with women. These didn't become poems but served as *bridges* to poems like "passage" (quoted at the beginning of this article), poems which were not especially feminist in focus. Since then, dreams have come to feed my life/work more and more.

Now, about the *process*. Jung said, *"Proceed from the dream outward."* OK, and sometimes that's easy, as in "On a Black Horse," which followed naturally from the dream experience. Yet the going isn't always so direct. More often you feel like a translator—how to deal with one dimension in a language that was evolved for another? How to translate the nongrammatical plasticity of time/space dissolve into daylight consciousness language? The language blurring problems in Quebec seem small compared to this! How can our verb tenses accommodate the past present future all-at-onceness of dream texture? How can we preserve the gestalt, respect the wholeness of the dream, which is a "poem" already, intact and alive, if we extract a portion of it? From the first word, we are editing, interpreting, making—like it or not—symbol out of image, and as Jungian James Hillman writes: "Dream is not symbol, it is image." Regarding this process of going from dream to prose or poem, Carol Leckner writes:

> I've learned that the two mechanisms (to write poetry and remember and record a dream) do not usually operate together, especially since the writing mechanism is filled with all sorts of necessities which govern a pleasing form, structure, rhythm, sound and narrative. The better a writer becomes, the better s/he is able to perfect these techniques, and then the techniques begin to become part of a subconscious apparatus of writing. The mechanism of remembering a dream, however, is to receive and recover. These two functions are quite different and most often there is a translation needed between the two, especially as dream sequences usually do not make sense logically.... That's when the forging of common aims and needs takes place. [3]

There are many ways of refining interior antennae so translation from dream to poem is easier. The first is faith in the validity of perceptions from the unconscious. I've found that any practices/doings that shift the focus of consciousness (meditation, shoulder stands, left hand writing, orgasm, recording of just-before-sleep "hypnogogic" visions) make the boundary between dream and daily logic more transparent—the kind of bleed-through of dimensions that Doris Lessing writes about in *Memoirs of a Survivor*. Once, before sleep, my left hand scribed these words, which I've since used as a dream amulet to suggest myself into greater dream receptivity and recall:

> I receive the rays with open heart
> images that flood me indream
> I will be clear when they come
> they will be true as the Sun

Use of the right hemisphere lefty has proved helpful in recovering dream images. (I no longer have to actually use the left hand but can click into left hand mind at will. And I wonder whether Memory is the bridge between the two hemispheres?)

We can be more attuned to dream with the playful riming punning intuitive non-grammatical less-critical less-well-behaved left hand. In "Whales," I related the contents of a newspaper clipping on whale "suicides" with the right hand. When I moved into the indream image, I switched to the left hand:

> standing on shore
> I am with someone
> and the whales are talking to us
> without words
> from the glassing sea
> . . .

Sometimes, despite work and subconscious suggestion, you're left with a fragment that may be evocative but is more "piece" (A. Gold!) than poem. As California poet Joanna Thompson puts it, "the apparatus for pulling material out of the dream is imperfect." This is especially frustrating when you hear or see a poem (or message or equation) indream, are aware you're dreaming and aware you want to keep it, wake up, the tones/lines still in your ears/eyes, grab pencil but the lines dissolve faster than you can get them ("green glass arabesques I couldn't catch"). Clayton Eshleman keeps pen and/or tape recorder by his bed, but the dreamer forgets all so quickly... Denise Levertov did succeed in capturing a whole poem from a dream. "Runes" (in *O Taste and See*) are the words of three ancient Finnish runes which indream, Levertov, as a child of eight or nine, was given to write out.

I once had a poem delivered indream on color TV on the six o'clock news by Walter Cronkite (no, he's not an Animus figure here!). A moving painting went along with the words. I was enchanted by the delicacy of the images. When the poem was over, Walter bade us Goodnight in his best Time/Life voice. All I could recall was the first line: "Here, spontaneity is praise," and some lines about yellow grass.

So this gets into the realm of Memory. Maybe one key is music; music does help carry memory (the bards with fifty-verse ballads). Students have told me of receiving whole songs indream. Shamans do, too. Then another key, I believe, is to cultivate our ability (though often latent) to hook into a "free awareness" state more and more often, in which we allow ourselves to let down our learned filters in order to receive more trans-time/space input, while remaining grounded in consciousness. Then creativity could become the rule rather than the extraordinary exception.

What emerges for me after years of fanatical dream journalling, aside from insight into my psyche, is a series of dream poems I call *Oneiros* ("dream figure"; the Greeks believed that dreams came to you as Someone, as Athene, or your father, say). Many of them deal with recovering information from the ocean and its creatures, or from horses (as in *Horses*):

from the deeps come helpers,
Serpent power I greet you
(from *Cobra*)

Neath the sea she sings,
O I am cloud, I am cloud!
(from *Ea*)

after the flood I walked the seashore
finding glass objects of great beauty
...
chunk of sea-worn glass
dark green, spiralic,
what message coded in its weight?...

We dreamlink horse and swan
What meaning white mammal/white bird joined?

These are the dream poems that I feel have meaning beyond the me-scape. They envision future harmony among creatures, or the possibility of subtler knowing than we now possess. They are "passages" into a new perception and as such, I'm glad I could recover them to share with all.

Footnotes

1. *East West Journal*, "In Search of the Dream People," Jeremy Taylor on the work of Herbert Noone and Dr. Kilton Stewart, Vol. 7, No. 5, (May 1977), pp 80-2.

2. From *The Black Rider and Other Lines*, privately reprinted in 1905. Crane's mother took him to religious revivals at the beach where he had terrifying dreams of black riders and black horses charging him from the surf.

3. *Sundance Community Dream Journal*, A.R.E. Press, Va. Beach, Va., Vol. 1, No. 2, (Spring 1977), p. 224.

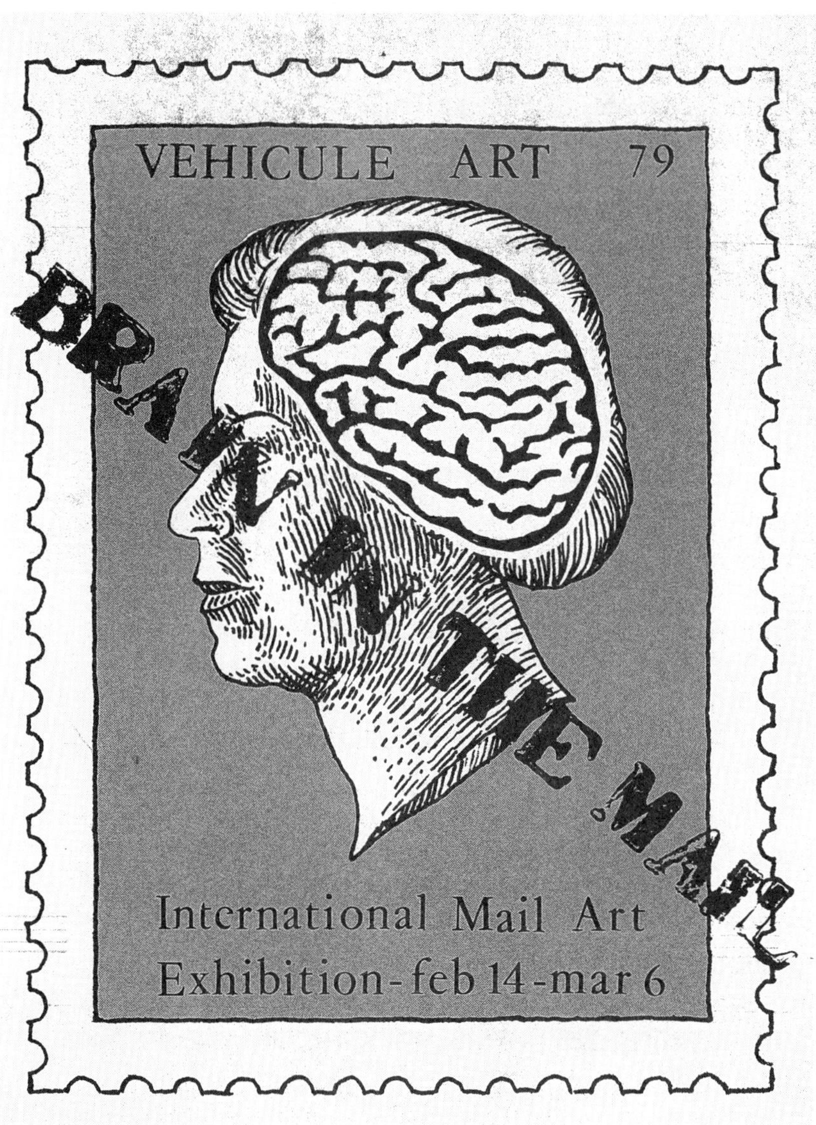
VEHICULE ART 79
International Mail Art
Exhibition-feb 14-mar 6

Poetry & Mind
Stephen Morrissey

Montreal Journal of Poetics 2:3-4, 1984

Henry Miller, in his novel *Sexus*, writes, "Everything external is but a reflection projected by the mind machine." This statement, if true, points to the necessity of a radical change in our understanding of the mind. If everything external is a projection of the conditioned mind, then everything we say or think about "reality" is a projection of our own self; everything we feel about "reality" is a projection—in every sense, "the observer is the observed."

A major activity of the mind deals in censoring the perceived world. It seems evident that the mind acts as a filter; we choose what we want to perceive and edit out the rest. Obviously there are different types of awareness. Chemical stimulants and depressants are commonly used to alter consciousness. Insects, birds, fish and many varieties of mammals perceive the world differently than humans.

We have chosen to develop the linear and intellectual abilities of the mind, but this has been done at great expense. We have narrowed consciousness so that we do not see the beauty of nature. This separation from nature is a part of our alienation from each other, from our feelings, and from a quality of mind that allows us to live harmoniously in the world. Many mystics, Christian, Hindu, Buddhist, Taoist, etc., as well as the shaman of so-called primitive people, tell us that there is an "undifferentiated unity" in all of existence: this unity of life has been lost to us.

That the ego, the self, the " I," has narrowed consciousness is obvious today; we cannot see the unity underlying all things. Instead, we see a projection of our fragmentation. We have reached a crisis in human consciousness, a crisis manifested in our utter disregard and contempt for living things. What are we going to do about it? Without understanding the way the mind works any action, any doing, will come from a fragmented mind and therefore result in a modification and perpetuation of the crisis.

There is an arrogance to those who rely on thought as the way to find "truth"; this is evident in the intellectual's approach. Increasingly we have come to rely on thought to understand "reality": it is believed that just about anything can be understood or known if we merely have enough information about what we are studying, Then we begin the process of speculating, analyzing, being rational, and theorizing. It is assumed that we *can* know, that not knowing is ignorance and that ignorance is a bad thing. Now we view institutionalized "education" as a life-long process, assuming that this type of education is a positive and good thing and that the teacher has important and necessary information to communicate. Underlying all of "education" is the presence of the authority, the one the student must please by modifying his behaviour. We are trained by our educational system to be aggressive and despite the appearance of scientific attitude our approach is anything but scientific. Science means to put things in their right order: that is, to observe without the ego, without preconceptions. But, we never really look, we glance; our observations are all from minds projecting an idea, belief, tradition, prejudice, etc., onto the thing observed. We know nothing but our own desires, needs, and thoughts; we are fragmented and alienated and in this is the violence underlying our activities.

Recently we had an electrician working at our house. He was looking for a broken wire and his approach was, "thought is always wrong." By this he meant that wherever he thought the broken wire would be found would be where it wasn't. He had to work from not knowing: any "knowing" was merely a projection of thought and had nothing to do with the broken wire itself. We have ideas, beliefs and opinions about everything and because of this we are separated from "reality." In the negation of what we "know" there is the possibility of learning of what we don't know.

We believe that by thinking, whether speculating or analyzing, we can arrive at truth, as though truth were an inflexible and permanent object to be grasped and held by the mind. A mind consumed with thought, whether it be in the form of belief, tradition, ideology, religion, etc., can not know truth, it can know only its own conditioned projection. When the mind is quiet then truth can come uninvited and unself-consciously. This quietist and passive way is the opposite of our aggressive approach. In the well-known story in Paul Reps' *Zen Flesh Zen Bones*, a university professor visits a Zen master who "poured his visitor's cup full, and then kept on pouring":

> "Like this cup," Nan-in said, "you are full of your own opinions and speculations. How can I show you Zen unless you first empty your cup?"

In Thomas Merton's autobiography, *The Seven Story Mountain*, there is an interesting character; Merton writes that Bramachari "was never sarcastic, never ironical or unkind in his criticisms; in fact, he did not make any judgements at all, especially adverse ones. He would simply make statements of fact, and then burst out laughing—his laughter was quiet and ingenuous, and it expressed his complete amazement at the very possibility that people should live the way he saw them living all around him."

How do people live that so amazed Bramachari? First, the spiritual dimension has been totally lost from our lives. Secondly, there is violence at every level of our existence: whether it is the violence of the single word spoken harshly, or the violence of international conflict, collectively and individually we live with the constant presence of violence. Living in William Blake's state of "experience," being disequilibriated both psychologically and physiologically, we have lost both a feeling of mystery when in nature and the happiness and joy that is alive in the child.

The experience of avoiding certain thoughts, or repressing thought, is a pleasurable one: there is a sense of going beyond the self while knowing that the self will still be there when one returns. The self, consumed with its everyday concerns, fears, anxieties, can easily escape self-consciousness through alcohol, drugs, sex, music, education, politics, sports, work, religion, reading, and other similar activities. But all of these ways of avoiding thought are still an act of the self; the motivation is to escape what is painful into what is momentarily pleasurable. Today, everything "external" has gained ascendancy of importance: but the external is a projection of the mind that is fragmented.

Boethius, in *The Consolation of Philosophy*, writes:

> The man who searches deeply for truth, and wishes to avoid being deceived by false leads, must turn the light of his inner vision upon himself. He must guide his soaring thoughts back again and teach his spirit that it possesses hidden among its own treasures whatever it seeks outside itself.

What is the "inner vision"? Isn't it intelligence, an awareness in which there is no intervention of thought with its confusion? To know ourselves is usually considered a process of thought and time; years may be spent in psycho-analysis or a monastery, often with few results. Dr. David Shainberg, in *Within the Mind of J. Krishnamurti*, writes, "...the process of thought is an escape from the immediate action of seeing."

The art of seeing or looking is the observation of what is. J. Krishnamurti, in *Education and the Significance of Life*, writes:

> To be creative is not merely to produce poems, or statues or children: it is to be in that state in which truth can come into being. Truth comes into being when there is complete cessation of thought; and thought ceases only when the self is absent, when the mind has ceased to create, that is, when it is no longer caught in its own pursuits. When the mind is utterly silent, without being forced or trained into quiescence, when it is silent because the self is inactive, then there is creation.

For those who work with words there is the possibility of confusing the word with the thing described just as many confuse "thoughts about reality" with "reality." There is no intrinsic value to words except as a means of communicating. Poetry, as with all art, has a very limited value. If we are to create something new then the old mind, burdened with fears and anxieties, must be transformed. A poetry and culture of the future must deal with the transformation of the mind. Are we trying to go beyond words in our poetry? Can we discover that which hasn't been touched by words? When we are caught in words, technique and Fashion, we have removed ourselves from the possibility of understanding what exists beyond words.

Collectively and individually we live with violence. To create a culture that is concerned with the transformation of the mind we might begin by saying that we don't have any answers. Until that time, which can be right now, all of our poetry will be involved with what is temporarily fashionable and with the aggrandizement of the self. No "great" poetry can be written until we look at life without the division and intervention of thought—but this requires love and consideration.

George Bowering reading at the John Abbott College art gallery, 1977.

On Not Teaching the Vehicule Poets

George Bowering

English language creative writing students in Montreal of the late sixties and early seventies, if they were serious about things, were up against a number of problems. English language poetry in Quebec had a history that was both nationally known and insular. As far as the Montreal flacks and interested partisans in the rest of Canada were concerned, Irving Layton was the big poet of his generation, and Leonard Cohen was the big poet of the next generation. Young poets looking for glamour in a poetry career were either enamoured of Cohen's example, or obstructed by it. Young poets looking for poetry were not given much of a chance to find it outside the local legends.

Put it another way: there were, according to Montreal literary scenarists, two major traditions of EngLang poetry, the Anglo line of Scott, Smith, Kennedy, Jones, and the magazines like *Northern Review*, and the Jewish mob led by Layton, but including Cohen (sort of) and the Laytonettes, Boxer, Hertz, Mayne, etc. Neither crowd was particularly noted for keeping up with what was happening in the U.S. and Canada. The Montreal world, self-inflated, was sufficient to itself. As will happen in such a situation, attention was deflected away from form and technique and directed toward personality and portrayal of the homeland.

The best antidote to such provincialism was the poetry reading series at Sir George Williams University, which started the year before I got there. It was organized by Roy Kiyooka, the prominent poet/painter who was teaching at SGWU at the time, and English professors Stan Hoffman and Howard Fink. Compared to the desultory reading series run at universities these days, it was a class act. The poets were flown to Montreal, met at the airport, lodged at the Ritz Carlton Hotel, given lots of attention and room service, a dinner, the reading, and a party that was not BYO anything. There were ten or twelve poets a year featured in that series, including Robert Duncan, John Newlove, Michael McClure, Margaret Avison, George Oppen and Daphne Marlatt. I have not seen its like in the two decades since then.

I assumed then and assume now that the opportunity created by that reading series did more for "my" writing students than anything I could have told them. But I did tell them a lot. I told them which poets and books I found it important to read. I told them how to make poems from language instead of attitude. I told them that if you had $2.10 to your name, you could buy a book of David McFadden's poetry for $1.95.

After I left Montreal in 1971, a bunch of young poets and other miscreants started a reading series at Véhicule gallery, and a press called Véhicule. Since that time hyperactive Ken Norris has been keeping the name in whatever part of the public eye turns to poesy in and around Montreal. The Vehicule people got a good thing going, and certainly filled a gap that existed in English language poetry in Quebec.

I had some of the Vehiculas in my writing classes at Sir George. I didn't know what I was getting myself into, a westerner with definite opinions about poetry and its sources, dropped into the middle of Layton country. Well, there was Louis Dudek, who did not quite fit into the Anglo tradition, and who was not a Jewish poet, though people often thought he was. He had been for a few decades a magazine-publisher, culture critic, and very unornamental modernist poet. He sat on couches in Anglo apartments and Jewish apartments. He had published Leonard Cohen and Lionel Kearns. When I arrived in Montreal the famous quarrel between Dudek and Layton was still raging.

But I didn't see Louis any more often than I saw everyone else. Everyone else saw everyone else, among the published, but out of my habitual element, I was taken aback to hear that at their parties they discussed everything but poetry.

So my creative writhing (as Newlove called it) classes. With my memory shot now, I cannot remember all the young poets I sat with, and sometimes I like to think that I had students, Endre Farkas, for instance, who probably never sat in my room. I know some of the people I subjected to the heat: Carl Law, Tom Konyves, Dwight Gardiner, Susan Landell, John McAuley, Artie Gold.

Dwight Gardiner and Artie Gold were two hotshot friends, both going bald in their early twenties, both wry and hip. I was pleased to see that of all things, they were both reading Jack Spicer and Frank O'Hara. In 1966 I had had to introduce Spicer to the hip poetry gang in Detroit! Now a year or two later, I find two kids who had found him and O'Hara somewhere. Wonderful. Because not only were Spicer and O'Hara obviously in the underground as compared to the poets known by professors and big presses—they were even the contrary found in that underground. They were a challenge to Olson and Creeley, and so on. Wonderful.

Of course, Gardiner published four books before he became an ethnolinguist among the Shuswap people in the Thompson Valley. Gold too published four books in his youth, and is now a middle-aged Selected Poet. In my classes Artie Gold would arrive every week with two huge bags—one containing enough food to get him through to mid-class break, and the other crammed with a couple hundred new poems. When it came to photocopying the students' poems for class argument, it was sometimes like pulling hens' snot to get material from some of the hobbyists and explorers of self, but it was like putting up a snow fence against an avalanche of Artie.

Tom Konyves was a sly European, offspring of big city Hungarian Jews, a touch of another kind of maturity in the long room. He knew he was a poet or something, but he didn't know whether what he wanted to make was poems. I told him that form was never more than an extension of something-or-other, and the materials he handed in were less and less comfortable on the page. My conservative side rose up to resist, always a good sign. Konyves started making things out of the paper itself. Then he started substituting for paper. Then he threw away his pen. I recognized his restless genius and said get out of here.

A few years later he got tired of reading that Pound's "In a Station of the Metro" was a perfect modernist poem. He got a bunch of poets down to a station of the Montreal Métro, the busiest, the transfer cross-road of Bérri-de-Montigny, and had them perform the poem there, for hurrying strangers who hurried by in many east end languages. All the while he videotaped the event. Last I heard he is a video doyen in Vancouver, still interested in poetry, but not poems all that much.

John McAuley, was a lot quieter than those guys. He was steady and productive. His poems became longer and more pared-down as he progressed. I didn't say a lot to him, or I didn't say it very loud. I recognized a quiet, dedicated poet, a man who wanted to spend his life making poems better and better. I have met a few poets like that around the country, people like David Phillips and Judith Copithorne. We don't know how much we need them.

I don't teach creative writhing any more, or rather I have done so only one semester since leaving Montreal in 1971. I think that maybe we all have jobs we can be expected to do *for a while*—edit magazines, review books, teach writing classes. Creative writing teachers are always quick to tell you they once had so-and-so in a class once. Hell, Earle Birney used to say he had me in a class. That's all right, but it should never be confused with influence or shaping of careers or anything like that. If I had anything to do with the emergence of Véhicule I will gladly acknowledge the acknowledgement.

Vancouver
July, 1993

DEAR MR. TILDEN,
12:11
PUBLISHED
HhDaDa
MINIMAL-LY
You too
can be
What goes up
must come down.
SMALL WORLD TOURS
green "direction" arrow indicates that the car is going up, your eagerness to help the writers (who have always been so wonderful to you) cannot be controlled. You push both call buttons. Now you've done it because, as the faithful
the elevatee saves the three seconds it takes for the door to close by itself. If, when you enter the car, the "direction" light is pointing in the way you want to go, then push "Door Close" first and your floor-selection button second. But if neither "direction" light is lit when the doors open, don't
Post
MBER 30, 1976
25 Cents
3:00
PR
FIN
7
RACES
! at that point, we came up with the idea that put us where we probably should have been in the first place.
Ruling:
HIM
Bull
a poem
in a
china
SHOP
sh sh
Normally, it's not the
You're the fifth person
IT.

An Interview with Tom Konyves

Your early poetry strikes me as being very much in the Montreal Jewish tradition of Klein, Layton, and Cohen. Were you very aware of those three poets when you were a young apprentice poet?

Textually, I was more concerned with the masters than the moderns. The reputation of Irving Layton would, from time to time, blow across a winter night's conversation, and Leonard Cohen was—almost/hardly—one of us. Their exploits and achievements were enumerated, more than their lines. I had read enough of Layton to recognize that volume doesn't rock and roll make. Cohen was the moody lover, unapproachable but for the spirit in his lines. I remember being very moved by *Beautiful Losers*. Klein was the last of the three I read, but by that time I was impatient with measured lines and measured values.

Your first book, *Love Poems*, fits very comfortably into the Montreal Jewish tradition. Was that a conscious intention at the time?

Not at all. I had no interest in being identified as a Jewish poet. Having escaped Hungary at age 9, I was eager to assimilate—embrace a new language, a new culture—and I did, with a passion. By the time I entered Outremont High of the Protestant School Board, I was singing *Joy to the World* and *God Rest Ye* with no less enthusiasm than the songs around the Passover table. Thanks to university, I learned to wrestle with traditional Christian heroes and their souls' progress, from Marlowe to Dickens, Keats to Blake, Yeats to Eliot, and back again, until Blake's visionary lines finally subdued me and pulled me through their wake. I awoke on the beach of a mystical poetry where I lay in wonderment and desire. After a couple of years of writhing on Blake's cross of the Imagination, I discovered Kabbalism, a grassroots mysticism I preferred, eventually expropriating some of its more suggestive, lyrical, symbolic language for poems. But not its religiosity. My initial struggle as poet was to find a voice, not a tradition. *Love Poems*, simply, was a first gesture of a young poet.

Your second book, *No Parking*, seems to be written by an entirely different poet altogether. The traditionalism of *Love Poems* is replaced by a spirit of radicalism. Looking back, how do you account for that change?

Writing *Love Poems* represented my first peek at a world away from books. With 20 copies under my arm, I left Montreal for Toronto, read the poems to six-odd diners in the courtyard restaurant of Hart House, lay low in Buffalo for a couple of weeks before leaving for New York City. There, I began to enjoy—I was living and breathing poetry—exploring the juxtaposition of the academic/traditional to the concrete/contemporary. In New York I felt free, accepted, encouraged. Significantly, interaction with other poets became as important as the writing. The turning point was coming back to Montreal and discovering that the *scene was ripe for the plucking*: I met Ken Norris who shared my enthusiasm for a new poetry *for us*. My friendship with Ken was to broaden until there were many of us, a *vrai* group.

Around this time I stumbled across the paintings and writings of Francis Picabia, which introduced me to Dada and its protagonists, Tzara, Ball, etc. When I began to juxtapose the playful, daring spontaneity I sensed in Dada with the visions of the contemporary, I discovered that the *futuristic, the avant garde* style of the '20s fit, even enhanced, the present.

Love Poems was a collection of my earliest poems. If there was any tradition that I wanted to fit into, it was probably a modern form of romanticism. By the time I wrote the poems for *No Parking*, I think I disowned the poet of *Love Poems*. I was weary of tradition; with each new poem I wanted only to confirm the validity of the contemporary and the unique.

You were part of the Vehicule Poets movement in Montreal in the late seventies; how did your participation in that group influence your writing?

At first, our get-togethers were spent in talking about poetry and socializing. We agreed on some basic principles: that the new poetry should reflect the new (contemporary) in content and form; that experimentation should be encouraged; that conservatism and traditionalism should be dismissed and openly opposed; and that poetry should reach its audience in a more immediate way. And then we said, "Let's go out there and dream."

We wrote easily, often, without too much pain. We watched our poems appear in public—the mimeographed *mouse eggs* was our poetry magazine—almost immediately after we wrote them. Poetry was alive, and Montreal was the right place. I was feeling the freedom poetry is after. My poems changed. Form could never have become so attractive in isolation; I was having serious fun! There were so many ways to express a poem that I began running, running until I ran off the page into visual performance, eventually video. I kept asking, what has not been done? Or, what have we not done?

The group was for the opposite of isolation, therefore it was inevitable that our poems would become one, that we would write collaborative poetry. As a matter of fact, the first night we really came together was when we followed a few beers with a blank sheet of paper which we passed around for a couple of lines. The support of the group certainly facilitated my efforts in collaborative work. The (one and only) performance of "Drummer Boy Raga: Red Light, Green Light" was satisfying partly because I initiated it, witnessed its evolution, saw it through to performance; but sharing a collaborative spirit was such a unique feeling that I continued working with other poets, artists, musicians for many more years. My performance orientation culminated in working in video, creating "videopoems," again with the support and participation of the others. We were friends.

Of all the Vehicule Poets you seem to have been the most influenced by European art movements like Dadaism and surrealism. The others seem to have been primarily influenced by hip American poets like O'Hara and Corso and Creeley.

I was influenced by Ginsberg, too. My trip to New York in '74 turned poetry around for me and the New York sensibility had a lot to do it. I had met poets from the west, and I was already familiar with Michael McClure, but my soul was somewhere between the triangle of New York's utter freedom, Montreal's French connection, and Toronto's middle English.

When I discovered Dada, my biggest surprise was that I hadn't known of it earlier. It fit well with the gallery art, with my cynical and de-constructive side, with the word permutations of Kabbala, with my love of word-play. Dada had played itself out primarily in French; I believed there was still unexplored territory in English.

You once commented that the biggest influence upon the Vehicule Poets was the gallery space—Véhicule Art—where they conducted their reading series. Why do you see that as having had such impact?

Once we accepted the fact that we were an identifiable group, we began to explore ways we could express ourselves: publishing magazines and books, broadsides and chapbooks on a frequent basis, collaborating/performing together, activities resulting from our common meeting space, the gallery.

As members, we vacillated between obsessed involvement in the gallery's affairs and utter boredom with it. Our reading series was a common responsibility, but the political gallery environment became equally effective in strengthening the bond between us, the poets of Véhicule. I can't overemphasize the significance of arriving at the space to find a thought-provoking, if not shocking, exhibition of young experimental artists, as well as meeting and getting to know painters, sculptors, musicians, performance artists, video artists, dancers from all over the world. The atmosphere was almost always intense, electric. It was inevitable that we would examine our own expression, poetry, in the light of what we were seeing around us.

As we became familiar with the operations of the gallery, we learned the advantages and disadvantages of organization. We also witnessed the use and abuse of power and politics. Unlike university faculty lounges, libraries and bookstores, the gallery made poetry come alive; it was more than just a venue for readings. (Coffee houses were different, but ultimately the poets there do not control the space. At Véhicule, we did.)

A donated printing press became Véhicule Press, through which we began to publish our books. The press, the performance/reading space, the video recording equipment, the gallery network, the resident and visiting artists, the communication tools (access to telephone, mass mailings, calendars, stationary), enabled us not only to participate in an active art scene, promote each other's work, and keep up to date on contemporary art issues, but also to take poetry wherever we desired... We became aware of the power of the group—allowing us to reach farther, inside and out.

You said that, in *No Parking*, "with each new poem I wanted only to confirm the validity of the contemporary and the unique." How did you go about doing that?

The poem as aesthetic experience is as unique for the poet as for the audience. The poems in *No Parking* were unexpected—they surprised me as much as anyone else.

Words have a way of falling into place which has nothing to do with poetry. Lionel Kearns once said, "Poetry is tricking words into saying something." When I first heard that, I thought, that's *exactly* what I've been trying to do. For me, one of the challenges of contemporary poetry was (and still is) the differentiation of poetry from prose. At the time, it seemed to me that poetry was the only way some writers would approach subjects dealing with emotions, relationships and minute observations. Sentences were chopped into lines, with or without punctuation. When I realized that these poems could be rebuilt into perfect sentences and paragraphs of prose, I knew that the new art of poetry required a unique method.

The poems in *No Parking* were attempts to create seamless collages of journalism and fantasy, brief streams of consciousness and deliberate wordplay, the colloquial and the penned, the visual and the audible, the specific and the abstract, the eternally sacred and the fleeting present, all ultimately the application of a Dadaist principle—the union of opposites.

After a few lines I decide I can't go on too much about this, there's something else happening, unrelated but simultaneous. Or, *something's got to be said for the other side*. The poem will then shift focus, in content or form.

Many of the poems are experimental, in that the contemporary vision is superimposed on traditional backgrounds, such as politics, religion, love, marriage, poetry, myth, art. In this process, the poem is constantly changing form to avoid capture and as a result, codification.

The effect on the audience is not meant to be satisfying. The poems lure the listener/reader into uncharted territories of experience, often too brief to be savoured without close examination.

How did you feel about how this work was received when the book was published?

The title poem had received some positive attention, having been performed many times and published in some anthologies of note, and I was pleased that the poetry community would get to see more of my work. I don't think I received many reviews, some were favourable, some not. It appeared that either what I was doing was not as radical as I thought, or it was simply beyond the audience's comprehension or appreciation. Now that's not meant to belittle the audience, but the truth is that experimental or non-linear poetry is not always *fun* for the audience. Some of the poems suggest new ways of experiencing poetry, some even question the very *nature* of poetry and, in the process, could (and probably did) alienate some people.

How was the video work you were doing different from what was going on in both poetry and video art at the time?

In 1977, poetry was still writing and reading. While some performance artists were experimenting with poetry at alternative galleries and performance spaces, the mainstream poetry scene was—not unexpectedly—print-oriented. The Canada Council, wielding significant power through grants to poets, defined poetry primarily by the publication of poetry in book form—48 pages minimum. While organizing a reading series at Véhicule, I had specific tasks: invite the poets, print posters, write press releases, set up chairs, introduce the reader, make coffee for the intermission, sell books, fill out forms for the poet to get paid and lock the doors after everyone left. Sometimes we set up the video camera and documented the reading. My interest in video began when I realized that once framed, the poet did not move out of the frame, and an audio recording could have served equally well. The medium of video was not being challenged or explored by poetry.

Poems were *for the page* and *for the ear*. There *were* poems *for the eye*—experiments in concrete poetry, conceived with the page in mind. Letters, words or phrases were blown up, cut up, strewn across the page, upside down, backwards, sideways, out of order, stenciled, outlined; typefaces were mixed, picture and text were juxtaposed; finally, collages appeared as poems. Minimalist art thus explored poetry and the experience of a poem.

The experimental artists at the time were fiercely interested in the non-narrative aspect of formalism, producing mostly conceptual works, culminating in not one but *two* new forms—*performance art* and *installations*.

The video artists were creating either conceptual works (video as fishbowl), bizarre exhibitionist fictions (performances created uniquely for the eye of the camera), or a combination of the two (video monitor as participant). I saw two distinct directions for poetry: towards the page and away from the page. Choosing the latter normally meant severing ties with the majority of poets, proudly flying the flag of radicalism, which ultimately meant being marginalized or simply ignored. The fact was that the mood was favouring the new (or so it appeared within the friendly confines of the gallery) and the medium of video was accessible. I approached video with concerns about the poet as performer as well as a trial ground for a novel treatment of text as *emotional texture*. I immediately liked the fact that, unlike the poem on the page, I was able to unravel the poem at my own chosen speed. What finally differentiated my videopoems from poetry and video art was this ability to simultaneously present a work and also question the role of the poet.

Do you think the video work you were doing had any affinity with today's music videos?

Yes, especially those music videos which utilize images seemingly unrelated to the lyrics. The superimposition of text over image is also relevant to the work I was doing.

While still producing videopoems you started edging into performance art. What prompted you in that direction?

In the process of creating videopoems, one of my primary concerns was with the role of the poet in the context of reading (in *Sympathies of War* I read sitting in profile, leaning in and out of the frame), performing (in *No Parking* I pace up and down on a loading dock), even the act of writing (in *Sympathies of War, a Postscript* I write one-liners on tear-off sheets).

What I was witnessing in the gallery as performance art was representative of what was most current, yet I still did not see poetry used as an integral part of the experience.

Performance art, unlike video, is based on the here-and-gone. Employing body language, the artist executes an action or gesture, the witnessing of which creates the work of art. My performance of Pound's "In A Station of the Metro" demonstrated that poetry can be *successfully* interpreted visually.

Experiments in poetry performances were natural extensions of the experiments in video. The content of the videopoems was a series of recorded performances. Performance was but another medium to explore in the light of poetry.

Tom Konyves performing "In a Station of the Metro," 1980.

***Poetry in Performance* attempted to document both your videopoems and your performance pieces. Why did you decide to translate these works into the conventional venue of the book?**

I was not actively pursuing the distribution of these works and I was concerned that if the videotapes ever disappeared, there would be no record of these works. The introductions and footnotes permitted me to take the audience "behind the scenes" to meet my many collaborators (and my sources).

In addition, the book format gave me the opportunity to describe not only the internal processes which gave rise to these works, but also the social, political, and artistic environment within which they were created.

I was also not blind to the fact that these works were on the fringe of the fringe and I earnestly wished to bring some of my experiences and discoveries to a mainstream public. This was also the motivation behind public projects such as *Poetry On The Buses* (1979), *Art Montreal* (1979-1980) and *The Great Canadian Poetry Machine* (1986).

***Ex Perimeter* almost hearkens back to *Love Poems*. Why was there such a significant change in your work?**

Ex Perimeter bridged my move from Montreal to the West Coast. The first of the three sections were written in Montreal, the last in Vancouver. Sandwiched between these are *Ten Poems around the Block*, poems about writer's block. The physical move was initiated by an emotional and spiritual one: I had met Marlene in Montreal in 1982. Six months later we were engaged and we flew to Vancouver to meet her family. The west coast was new to me and the grandeur of the surrounding mountains took my heart away. When we returned to Montreal, I realized that the coming change in my life was going to be monumental. Settling in Vancouver, my mind was on family, subsistence, beginnings. Some of the poems in the book reflect this *practical* side.

Literally wed to traditional values, I resolved to enrich the traditional *poetic* values of *meaning* and *craft* while not losing sight of having spent years on the other side of the fence: the young rebel experimenting with form and media, deconstructing language, intoxicated with irony.

While I was assembling the poems for *Ex Perimeter*, I did manage to write and perform one experimental work, *Motions*, using video, one slide, and electrical tape. My production dropped to six or seven poems a year, and with the pressures of my daily life I have found it extremely difficult to devote more of myself to poetry.

How do you feel today about experimental writing?

There is so much to be done, I wish I had the time to do it. I don't know how much (or how little) experimental work is being done. A couple of years ago, I went to an evening of "Performance poetry" and did not witness 10 seconds of "Performance." There was poetry, music, some sound poetry, hoopla, and smoke. No one waved a flag or a handkerchief, a sword, a gun, a pen, a feather or a finger.

Two years before that, I stood in the back row of a classroom filled with poets of the League, workshopping on "Performance poetry." Following the opening panel discussion, there were two "performances." I did not witness 10 seconds of "Performance." I chose an appropriate point in the question and answer period and after a brief historical review, vehemently objected to the travesty I had just witnessed and challenged all those present to argue for the validity of these "performances." The response was utter silence and some awkward laughter, like the perennial "oh no, here goes Tom again about video" I used to hear at League meetings, which I interpreted as "I know we should step into the twentieth century, accept the present and express the present through means of the present... but, Tom, does it have to be right now?"

In other words, experimental writing is only appreciated by a close-knit group, and they whisper their secrets to one another until someone cries out to be heard; and when they are heard, there are no whispers, only silence. When there is applause, you can be sure there will be wine and cheese later.

Do you consider yourself to be a west coast writer or a Montreal writer?

Montreal. Montreal.

What do you think about the current Canadian poetry scene?

I wish it was unfolding on Eighth Avenue, recorded on Sixth, broadcast live every Sunday at midnight, coast to coast.

Vancouver, BC
December 15, 1992

PROVERBSI #27

An audience is a dead performer reincarnated to applaud.

Endre Farkas recording "Public/Private" by Yves Bouliane, 1979.

Relationship:
An Interview with Endre Farkas

Essays on Canadian Writing 43, Spring 1991

Endre Farkas was born on March 11, 1948 in Hajdunanas, Hungary. He left Hungary with his family during the 1956 uprising, moved to Canada, and has lived in the Montreal area ever since. He teaches at John Abbott College. His books of poetry include *Szerbusz* (1974), *Murders in the Welcome Café* (1977), *Romantic at Heart and Other Faults* (1979), *From Here to Here* (1982), and *How To* (1988).

Your two major poetry collections, *Romantic at Heart and Other Faults* and *How To*, devote a lot of space to poems concerned with relationships. Do you think this is one of the primary touchstones of your work? Why?

Relationships are one of the primary touchstones of all our lives. We spend most of our lives seeking them, participating in them and often trying to get out of them (sometimes desperately). It seems to me that we (human beings) are relationship driven. Perhaps this is because we are forced to live a solitary existence due to our imprisonment in our bodies and minds. Most people can only handle this solitude for a little while and then it becomes loneliness, which is scary, so we seek company.

The poetry that I read and was excited by, at the start, was the poetry of the Beats. Aside from their loudness, they were confessional in the best sense of the word. The "I" was invoked not as an egoistic boost of "look at me!" but as a celebration of the individual in a world where conformity, uniformity, and corporate mentality were encouraged. It was poetry where what was going on in your personal life was material for poems. They were into their Beat lives. The sixties (my Beat times) was a communal time, and I participated in that, socially and individually. So I was into relationships and they were important, so I wrote about them and continue to do so. But I hope that when people read my book they'll see that I'm not, by any means, just writing about one kind of relationship. I am involved in relationships with men, women, children, parents, poets: the world.

In *How To*, you seem to work a lot with home-renovation metaphors. I take it this is meant to be read on more than just the literal level.

Yes. But before I comment on the other level, I want to say something about the literal level. It's to be taken as seriously as any other. In fact, the other levels can only really be appreciated if the surface is read and heard for what it is.

One of the things many of my generation were doing was leaving home and moving into communal-type situations. And because of the ideals and financial reality, we moved into old houses because they were cheap. They were absentee-landlord duplexes and triplexes, and the like. They also were appealing because of high ceilings, big windows, and wood floors. They invited renovating. It went with the ideology of doing it yourself. I like the notion of being able to do things for myself. It has become a trendy thing to do, but with the difference that you hire experts to do it for you. I used to have romantic notions about the craft. Of course, not having had a teacher, except necessity, I've had to learn how to on the job, and when time is not on your side (as it often was not), it can lead to frustration and anger. This frustration and anger spills over into other areas of your life. It becomes a metaphor.

And once you've done the job, you step back and sigh with satisfaction and relief of accomplishment. But this is tempered by expertise gained that allows you to see the flaws. You then try to appease yourself with the thought that you now have the know-how to do it properly, and promise yourself that next time it'll be perfect. And of course the next job gives rise to a whole new set of problems that you're not prepared or equipped for. So you start again from scratch. It's like relationships and poetry. I am still seeking the perfect fit, on all levels.

The other thing about the metaphors: they are not metaphors. They are the language of renovation. It is only after reflecting on, and expressing these experiences through poems that they become metaphors. In the poems, the language of renovation becomes charged, and triggers image connection for writer and reader.

How do you feel about the relation between poetry and domesticity? It seems to me that in your work you're often trying to highlight what's poetic in the everyday.

This aesthetic is again based on the literal understanding that I have been in a relationship for 18 years that has gone through a lot—from romance to parenthood. One does not preclude the other, but the intensity and focus do, over that time, certainly change. There are dramatic moments in our lives that are earth-shattering, death defying, heroic, and/or tragic. They are profound and effect us deeply. However those are *moments*. The rest of the time is the routine, the taking care of business. For me, surviving the routine is heroic, and seeing those routines and tasks as rituals is important; it puts things into perspective, and helps me to see what is worth doing. By celebrating them in poems, I try to convey their importance in the large scheme of things. Because they are in poems, they become more than just domestic chores: they become vital. It is also a political perspective, because from this point of view it is not only the grand and the powerful, but the ordinary acts and people that are relevant.

One of the most striking pieces in *How To* is "Letter to A.M. Klein." Klein seems to be an important figure to you. Why?

I don't know if we would get along, but I find that there are a lot of similarities between us. We are both children of Jewish, Eastern European immigrants; we grew up in the same neighbourhood; we both became poets and tried/try to maintain a normal life as well. Both of us have moved away from our parents' traditional faith (not without its consequences). Also, his lyrical tone and social conscience strike a sympathetic chord in me. He is, I think, Canada's first urban and urbane poet. He loved language, and liked to play with it. Klein was at ease with his Montreal, and didn't seem to have a second thought about making it an important part of his poetry. He tried to map its sacred geography as Joyce mapped Dublin. He celebrated (in the Catholic sense of the word) his place, even if at times it drove him to depression. By the way, one thing I don't want to have in common with him is his fate.

How do you feel about being an English poet in Quebec? Do you think you have any kind of specific role to fulfill?

I am not an English poet in Quebec. I am a poet writing in English in Quebec. This to me is an important difference. I have an immigrant background, and English is not my mother tongue. I do not have any guilt complexes about being part of an elite ruling class. I do, however, share a sense of isolation and alienation with the other poets writing in English in Quebec. There are many reasons for these feelings. First of all, we were preceded by very high-profile writers such as Scott, Klein, Layton, and Cohen. They established Montreal as *the* English poetic centre of Canada. Ironic, when you think of it: they do parallel Montreal's financial rise and decline. In the late sixties and early seventies, we witnessed the metamorphosis of the French Canadians into Quebecois, and the shift of economic and poetic focus to Toronto. I say we "witnessed" because most English writers in Quebec felt themselves to be outside of what was happening. They didn't feel that they belonged to the English establishment, they sympathized with the Quebecois but could not deny their own linguistic or cultural roots. Most did not want to, or could not, write about what was happening. But because of my ethnic background and friendships (some of my best friends are "pepsis") I did. Most of my political comments were in the form of performance pieces such as *Face-Off/Mise au jeu* in 1980 (referendum time).

I had earlier, as an organizer of readings at Véhicule, tried to establish a bilingual reading series but was turned down by a francophone poet who was running a series. He said it was not politically correct. Six years later, I did organize a bilingual magazine reading series with Lucien Francoeur and Claudine Bertrand. So when we were beginning to publish, go public, the focus was on francophones. They were the ones the rest of Canada was curious about. That is all well and good, but when the corollary to that is that there is no notice of the English writing community, then you become frustrated. This frustration is exacerbated by being shut out from the local media. All this can really give you a sense of being an island within an island within an island. It's a lonely job, but somebody's gotta do it! As to having a specific social role to fulfill, yes and no! To write.

For the past number of years you've been running The Muses' Company/la compagnie des muses, an active literary press. What kind of goals and objectives do you have as a literary-press publisher?

Aside from publishing high-quality material (a goal of all literary presses) I focus on new, fresh voices. Most of the books I've published are from Quebec. This is partly a conscious aesthetic decision and partly a practical one. My list of publications seems to include writers who are neither from the French nor English community. My fraternity with the immigrants and exiles is again perceivable.

Back in the 1970s, you were associated with Véhicule Press and were one of the so-called Vehicule Poets. What was that all about? Do you think that movement made any substantial impact on Canadian poetry?

It was an unconscious reconstruction of a rundown scene. It was about alternatives. It was about being young and naive and thinking we would live forever. It was about late nights, good sex, and dope. It was about a new phase in literary activities. It was about taking chances. It was about serendipity. It was about friendships. It was fun. Our aesthetic was as varied as the individuals. There was Artie Gold's American hip, [Tom] Konyves's videodada, [Claudia] Lapp's spiritual eroticism, [Stephen] Morrissey's Zen conceptualism, [John] McAuley's concrete, Norris's democratic encouragement, and Farkas' sound-movement performance pieces. Maybe (Konyves suggests this, and I tend to agree) our working out of an alternative gallery, primarily occupied by visual artists on the fringe, encouraged us to experiment and try to merge the word with other media. I don't know if we were a movement, but we certainly were interested in being kinetic.

As for impact on Canadian poetry, because a lot of our work was off the page, it didn't get past the moment during the event. Aside from Ken, we weren't prolific producers of books. Also, because conservatives are in power, and not only in politics, we are, right now, a footnote. I certainly think we're worth much more. And it wasn't for lack of effort. I don't think that there was any other group of poets anywhere in this country involved in as many, and as varied, collective activities. We ran readings, published books, collaborated on performances, produced videos, put poems on the buses, on the dance floor, and on [record] albums. We certainly had an impact on the Montreal English writing scene. We certainly made enemies.

Your first book, *Szerbusz*, was about a return trip to your native Hungary. Did that return home have a major impact on your work? Do you think of yourself as an expatriate Hungarian writer, or as Canadian?

That book is my ethnic roots book. It's my you-can't-go-home-again book. That is a quick synopsis. The longer one is more interesting and more likely the truth. Szerbusz is a Slavic salutation meaning both "hello" and "good-bye." I escaped Hungary with my parents during the 1956 uprising. I was only eight then, and when I arrived in Canada, it seems that I integrated very quickly. I didn't get assimilated, but neither did I get ghettoized. In 1972 I had the opportunity to go back for a visit, and I consciously made a decision to write a book of poems about it. I went back on two levels: as one born in that country and going back to visit relatives, and as a poet-observer-recorder. The circumstances under which we left, and my being very young, made leaving a decision I did not take. It was taken for me. Going back was a very conscious act taken by an adult. I felt that I had to go back and say "szerbusz." It was something I had to do; it had to be the first book. It was almost as if I had to get things straight with people and places and ideologies and mythologies. I came to see my home as a place in which my family was persecuted. So on that level I don't have much love for it. However, I also had a feeling of belonging, [of] being on native soil where firsts happen and forever shape an important part of the consciousness. I sniffed at their lives and sensed a familiarity. However, I also knew that I was no longer one of them. I was a stranger who could often detach and watch the goings-on. This mix made me feel like an exile. And so I guess this feeling makes me a writer in exile. And as a writer in exile, I sense that we are all exiles—especially in Canada.

In *Szerbusz* there are several encounters with Gypsy culture in Hungary. Did this have any impact on you in a major way?

My mother told me that I was wet-nursed for a while by one. So I've got a bit of Gypsy in me. It started out as a curiosity. I had been told stories by my parents about the Gypsies, and vaguely remember contact with them. The feelings most Hungarians have about Gypsies are akin to those white racists have about blacks: they're lazy, shiftless, drunkards, immoral fornicators, beggars, liars, and thieves who have rhythm. In many ways they are innocent of the world. This is interpreted as ignorant. The real problem is that Gypsies are/were nomadic in body and spirit and that's in conflict with any kind of bureaucracy, especially hard-line socialist. So they have been seen as unequal, and treated almost like slaves. I wrote a few poems about them. I tried to capture what they're really like, not only by the content, but by the use of lyrical lines and images that would evoke their sensibility.

This curiosity has led me to the poetry of Karoly Bari, a young Gypsy poet who has come to prominence in the last 10 years. I've been slowly and painfully translating his work. Again it's the outsider to whom I am drawn.

Your long poem, "Murders in the Welcome Café," reads like a kind of perceptual mystery. What were you trying to achieve by linking poetry with the detective genre?

Good question. As much as I knew what I wanted to do in *Szerbusz*, that's how little I knew what "Murders" was about. I was coming at it from the other end of the creative spectrum. Actually it was coming at me. I didn't write this poem. In the best Zen and romantic notions of creativity, it wrote me. Mystery was at the centre of this poem from the title to the last line. A number of things came together to make this poem. First of all, Artie Gold had turned me on to Raymond Chandler. His language moved me the way Lafleur dazzled and frightened goalies. It was his language that did it. It was a summer night, the kind of night that zaps you with déjà vu. I was walking past a corner Chinese restaurant, the kind only Chinese go to: a neighbourhood chop-suey joint. It was called the Welcome Café. I had a déjà vu. It was that murders were committed there. Four years later the poem was finished.

It strikes me now that the entire process is imbued with the detective genre. After the initial revelation of the crimes, the solution (the expression of it) seemed to be an unsolvable mystery. I had no idea where it was leading to. I tried to force its shape and voice and images through logical means. Only when I let go of it did it feel right. Then an irrationality would take control and part of the mystery would be solved. Images from the hard-boiled detective genre would be set in a recognizable, but skewed setting. I love the last line in the poem because it is such a classic cliché and yet, at the same time said something important about the poem and poet. "If you want me / I'm in the book." It is in the realm of a déjà vu. The detective genre was reinvented for poetic purposes. It's a postmodern detective poem.

Do you think that there is any kind of antipathy between poetry and popular culture? I ask this because you seem to work with metaphors and images drawn from popular culture quite a bit.

I think there is a complex relationship between the two. There is a love-hate affair going on. First of all, we are bombarded with manufactured pop culture 24 hours a day. And even though (or should that be "because") it is often simpleminded and naive it reaches billions, while poetry, for the exact opposite reason, reaches only hundreds. For Greeks, popular culture included their gods, their wars, their sports. That's what they wrote about. Shakespeare wrote about queens, kings, plots, lovers, human nature—pop culture of his times. In both examples, they took their pop cultures and elevated them to art. I try to do that.

The big difference between then and now, I think, is that in those times, poetry, theatre, and (later) books, were also the pop culture, and of course that is not the case today. That is what poetry today is resentful of. Poets of my generation in North America were the first to get so pop cultured. From TV to flickering TV we (en masse) got pop cultured on the same stuff. We have a collective pop-culture mythology to which we allude, and use for images, metaphors, and symbols. People love it, even though they can see it for what it is. It is also unrequited, and, as the song says, "unrequited love's a drag and I've got it pretty bad."

You once described your muse as being the wrestler Killer Kowalski. Does this in any way reflect how you view the process of writing?

Often. Because nowadays most poets do not consciously write to a given topic, but respond to urges; writing is a process of letting go. Killer Kowalski appears in a poem that is about the struggle to overpower the force that stands in the way of the poem and make it give it up. I hadn't been able to write for a while, and I felt frustrated and angry. This poem exploded in one sitting. I then went back and fixed it up. The only belief I hold true about the writing process is that the poem only works when the form and content intertwine like lovers, and their being one is "it." By form I mean structure as well as language. So Killer in that poem has to wipe out the ego to let the poem come through. What I most like about this poem is that the muse is male. I wrote this in the early seventies. It was one of my earliest liberated poems.

In the early eighties, you were very involved in performance art and working with people from other disciplines. Why did you suddenly feel the need to have your poetry move beyond the page?

There were a number of reasons. One was the influence of Véhicule Art Gallery and the visual artists who were getting into all sorts of crossovers, coming up with performance art. Another was my wife's involvement with Contact Improvisation and her support and interest in working together. After years of running reading series, my boredom with straight readings led me to question the validity of these performances. That's what readings are, but both the reader and listener pretend that it's not. We all know poets who can save bad poems with their rambling erudition and/or well-inflected voices, etcetera. I also found it very uptight and conservative. In a way, moving into performance poetry was a getting away from the literary community. I had also been interested in concrete poetry for a while. My take on concrete poetry was that the visual poet was attempting to move past the static state of the words on the page. I played (I use "played" deliberately) with images, and in them it was movement that I seemed to be after. In "Time through Trains," an early, lengthy narrative poem, I shaped verses in the form of trains, towns, and comic-strip balloons. I also put them on a model train and videoed it. It was a literal attempt to make the poem concretely kinetic.

We talk of breath in poetry, but it's not really clear what we mean. Working with dancers (and taking classes) I realized that they had to know. Their art depended on it. So I started experimenting. I went back to the source. Often I'd start performances with breathing:

as the breath is the journey
I move
and it is imperceptible as
is the breath
just breathed in
and
out

This breathing I'd make audible, and out of it shape words. In a way I was exploring one of the sources of language: the biological component. I tended to create minimal texts with modular structures. Sounds, words, phrases would be repeated in different ways: sequence, pitch, persons, positions. A dancer lying on his/her back will say a phrase differently than one who is running or jumping or carrying someone. These changes could also affect how the audience reacts. We did a performance, "It Runs in the Family," which we started off in the dark with Michel Bonneau and me breathing very softly and slowly and working up to audible breathing (it took about three or four minutes). Before we could go on to the text, we realized that someone else was heavy breathing with us. A person in the audience got caught up in the breathing, and was now freaking. Instead of going on with the text, we breathed with her and brought her back to normal breathing. This incident changed/charged the performance. I couldn't have affected anyone like that with poems on the page.

Endre Farkas and Michel Bonneau in "The Heart of the Matter," 1982.

My performance work has made me look quite carefully and differently at the words I put on the page. I check how a poem scans on the page by reading my poems out loud to hear how they sound. [Roy] Kiyooka told me he does the same.

Musically and movement-wise, you can see similar modular explorations in the work of postmodern dancers and musicians like Lucinda Childs and Philip Glass. I was being exposed to their...work [and that of others] through my connection with [my wife], Carol [Harwood], and Contact Improvisation. Also, working with Michel Bonneau (actor-musician) gave me insight into the theatrical possibility and effectiveness of words. I would write a text filled with adjectives and adverbs, etcetera. He would then work at paring it down to the essential. I found this helped me when I wrote for the page. By the way, I continued writing poems for the page, but not for publication.

Also, for me, it was a time of collaboration. A time for coming together in a time that seemed to be coming apart, especially in Quebec. I worked with francophones and anglophones in performances at a time when there was a push to divide.

Have you made any attempt to document your performance work in book form?

I have wanted, and started to, but it's slow work. I've had a title in mind for about eight or nine years. "Chance Takes" is what I want to call it, because it is about taking chances as well as playing with chance and doing takes. So the title is great and perfect, but putting it together is still in process. I want it to include not only documentation of the performances, but also of the visual and chance poems and pieces I've done in the past 15 years. Technically, this is a difficult book because I don't think it should be a traditional book. The form itself should be chance taking. So I'm playing around with book shapes and forms. I've got one in mind, but until I do it I don't want to say what it is.

All of your books seem to have a thematic consistency; that is, they don't read like collections of poetry. Are you very conscious of trying to put a book together as a coherent whole?

Yes. But I don't know when it starts. At first, the poems are individual moments. I don't see them as part of a greater plan. After I have a bunch of poems that I feel good about (which usually takes a couple of years), I start thinking of putting a manuscript together. At this point, I start thinking about a title that sounds good. It just seems natural to call it something. Give it what PVT [Peter van Toorn] calls "a handy handle." It now has a name, which sort of gives it a human quality. A golem with a soul. The title seems to invite other poems, and so it evolves. In my last book, I've included a couple of bridge poems: poems that were consciously written to be a bridge from one section to another. And then there are endings. Again, they have to feel right. Looking back with 20/20 hindsight, you might say that the approach to my putting together books is perhaps a metaphor of what I want to do in my life. Make some sort of order out of chaos. Maybe in the next book I will abandon all attempts at that and let chaos be, and see what that's all about.

As an editor of poetry, first at Véhicule Press, now at the Muses' Company, how do you try to help an author realize a manuscript?

I first have to be blown away by the spirit of the work. And; since one of the mandates I've given the press is to publish new writers, I feel that close work with the author is necessary. I do a close read, and ask questions about what isn't clear. I like to understand what I'm reading, so I usually start with sense: grammar, syntax, punctuation, etcetera. Then I read for phrasing, imagery—the freshness or staleness of them. I will often suggest rewrites, cutting out (trying to point out where I think the poem is). Also, of course, I will suggest poems to exclude, and perhaps reorganize the order. This kind of exchange is not only necessary, but it is one of the benefits. This discussion will go all over the place: from things that are directly relevant to the manuscript, to topics that are totally irrelevant, yet somehow essential to understanding the writer and his/her aesthetic. Where and when else will you get this kind of focus on the work?

How do you feel about the current state of Canadian poetry? What do you think of the work of your contemporaries?

I'm kind of numb to everything right now. I feel overwhelmed by the quantity. There is a lot of Canadian poetry, and that, in the long run, is probably good. It is an extremely busy world, and one that is no longer in danger of extinction. Of course, this does not mean that it is in any way of any use in our society. But that is its use: the arts are the only fields of human activity in which something is done for its own sake. The arts are one of the positive, unique features of the human race. It's what makes us special.

Politically and poetically, the times they are conservative. I'd like to see more passion in our work. I sense too much reason and competence. I'm not yearning for the past, but for a future in which we continue to take chances.

Left to right: Helen Clark, Andrew Harwood and Peter Bingham in "Sound Bodies," 1980.

Vehicule Days

Claudia Lapp

Being old enough to look back 20 years at my young adulthood makes me somewhat uneasy. Resistance is encountered because I don't want to wax nostalgic about those exciting years; and there's the fear of having no comment or opinion on the subject that would interest anyone other than the players involved. Like who cares about that small piece of the century's history other than us?

Still, one of the tasks of the poet is to remember; so, in an attempt to loosen the rust from my memory, I've been staring at the black and white cover of *The Vehicule Poets*, 1979. It shows the septet of us sprawled on a plank floor, Endre irreverent on one end, Steve schoolboyish on the other. The photo doesn't jar my memory that much, just makes me ask how it was that 2 Hungarians, 2 Americans (one German-born), and 3 native Canadians (2 Montreal-born) were able to create the poetry collective/gallery/performance space called Véhicule which became an important literary nexus in Montreal in the 1970s.

When I look back into that time, I come up with a jumble of feelings and no particular theme. What I do know is that Montreal has always been my poetic home and Vehicule my "tribe." Since returning to the States (the year of the photo) and searching for home in West Virginia mountains and Maryland suburbs and having found it last year in the Willamette Valley of Oregon (increasing the number of Vehicule poets on the West Coast to 2, with Tom in Vancouver), I was never again able to find a group context for my poetic soul. Not that we Vehicule poets were an entity as much as seven distinct voices, but we had a physical space around which we could spin and we appreciated and encouraged each other and pushed each other in a loving, non-competitive way.

Since I left Montreal, I've worked with individual poets, always women, teaching and performing, but have never been able to hook into a creative collective like Véhicule. I've truly missed that, because I tend to be lazy without some prodding and, though I cherish and need solitude more and more to create, having the feedback and example of different minds around me is what has always stretched me beyond old boundaries. My most steady poetry partner for the past decade has been Linda Joy Burke. Her intensely political voice balances my more introspective one and catalyzes joint readings around women's issues, green vision, and peace (we did a reading right after the Gulf War that was very healing for us, as well as the audience).

I've been thinking about being the sole female in Véhicule. Of course I loved it. My female ego enjoyed the strokes and, unlike so many feminists of the 60s and 70s, I didn't have an ax to grind with men. I never felt like the "token" woman: I just happened to be in the right place at the right time to become part of this dynamic circle of writers. I was able to freely express my developing personal brand of feminism that drew heavily on non-Western/Buddhist archetypes as well as the more familiar Western mythology. I always felt that my tribe welcomed that vision. I did have several close female poet friends—Janet Kask, Anne McLean, Carole TenBrink, Carole Leckner—and they were among the poets who presented at the gallery.

I also recall how much we (Vehicule) did, en groupe: publishing, recording, group readings, and the weekly reading series. We published Véhicule Press, Eldorado Editions, Maker Press and mag, to name a few. Michael Harris and I kicked off the first weekly reading series, shivering in our coats in the unheated space that first Sunday at 61 Ste. Catherine. A journal entry reminds me of a group reading on April 9, 1977 (Moon in Capricorn). Endre, Ken, Tom, Opal Nations and Claudia read at the Ethan Allen Engine House #4 in Burlington, Vermont, a space distinguished by molded white fiberglass chairs. I loved Tom's reading of *No Parking* then as I do now, in 1993. And there's the LP recording *Sounds Like*, which includes poets other than the seven of us and which I recently shared with the editors of *Silverfish Review* here in Eugene.

As I turn those years over in my mind, I also begin to recall the voices which were heard at the gallery over the years, not just Montreal poets but those from the West—Daphne Marlatt, Penny Kemp, Roy Kiyooka, Gerry Gilbert, Anne Waldman...I long to have a cassette that would gather all those Voices.

Why were we able to pull it off, then and there? We were young and living in a milieu of pre-rap, flower power euphoria without the political intensity of the U.S. with its string of assassinations and riots (it seemed less intense to us Americans, at any rate). The economic support for writers from the Canada Council turned manuscripts into books and paid us handsomely for readings (I've never been so well-paid for reading in the U.S., not even close!). And let's not forget that in those days it was still possible for a poet without teaching or Master's degree to be hired by the CEGEPs. So there were a lot of us poets gainfully employed teaching literature rather than working in retail.

Twenty years later, my poetry tribe continues to be Vehicule. The editors among us (Endre and Ken) continue to track us down over the years and miles, to coax writs from us. Though my ambitions have mellowed—I enjoy living room sharing as much as larger, public events—a part of me exists in a time and space that was possible for a decade or so, then, in Montreal, and that part of me is there, dancing, hair flying. I like to fantasize that the seven of us will have a reunion in the mid 90s in someone's backyard, or maybe camping out in a mess of tents by a mountain lake in the Cascades of Oregon. A marathon talk/poetry fest, seven from the Pluto in Leo generation meeting sans purpose other than hanging out together to see what could emerge from us once again sharing the same turf.

Claudia E. Lapp
1/8/93
Full Moon, Eugene

Claudia Lapp, 1993.

Artie Gold and Endre Farkas at The Word Bookstore, 1990.

John McAuley reading at Foufounes Electriques, 1985.

An Interview with Stephen Morrissey

As a young writer you were very interested in concrete and sound poetry. Why the interest, and what did you learn from your explorations?

What I learned was how to write poetry that communicates what I want to say to the reader. But that wasn't my intention when I began writing so-called experimental poetry. I thought experimental poetry was the destination and not just the path to something else; it was really my apprenticeship as a poet. If you had asked me why I write experimental poetry back in 1969 or the early 70s I would have come up with all sorts of theories. Obviously, I've evolved over the intervening years. The approach to poetry by experimental poets is still with me; that is, I am always taking risks in my work, I never censor what I write although I do substantial revising, and I am always changing in my work. But as far as the experimental theories, of so-called language poetry, or what have you, I'm really not interested in an intellectual approach to poetry.

In the 1970s you were part of the Vehicule Poets movement in Montreal. In your view, what was that all about?

That was all about setting up readings at Véhicule Art Gallery every Sunday afternoon for five or six years, meeting poets, being part of a loosely held together group, getting involved with poets, being committed to poetry and writing as a way of life. That's what it was for me, a place where I was accepted as a young poet who did experimental poetry and I would certainly not have been accepted by the other English-speaking poets in Montreal that had their roots in the early 60s scene, or what was left of it. In the past I have perhaps underestimated our work at Véhicule Art. This came home to me when I visited *Véhicule Art Inc.: Research in Progress*, an exhibition at Concordia University. We poets took over the gallery every Sunday afternoon, usually got a pretty good audience for whoever was reading, staged large group readings, brought in some big names in poetry, and were an important part of the life of the gallery. Our reading series at Véhicule Art was the most important poetry series in English-speaking Montreal at the time.

Another important thing about Véhicule was that we all worked in different areas of poetry but there was respect for each other's work. And I think we were influenced by the visual art that was shown at the gallery. It was a really creative time for us. Frankly, I miss the group spirit very much; I remember those years at Véhicule Art with fondness and nostalgia.

A few of the Vehicule poets were editors at Véhicule Press for about six years, during which time your book *The Trees of Unknowing* was published by Véhicule. Do you think that book in any way reflects the group aesthetic?

Was there a group aesthetic? I don't see how my first book reflected the group aesthetic. *The Trees of Unknowing* was the outcome of a gradual transition from contemporary ideas of experimental writing to a more traditional form of poetry. If there was any sort of influence between poets at Véhicule it was more in line of encouragement and acceptance of what you wanted to do in your work. We weren't Black Mountain poets, *Tish* poets, Beatniks, or what have you. For instance, Henry Miller was an influence; the work of J. Krishnamurti is important to me. Various visual artists also influenced my work, plus Chinese T'ang Dynasty poetry, photography, music, and so on. But I doubt these were influences on anyone else's work but my own.

For the most part, I haven't been too involved in the politics of poetry. A grant or a prize gives a certain amount of recognition, and this helps one to continue writing, but it has little to do with excellence in poetry. So, perhaps the Vehicule poets haven't made any lasting mark on Canadian poetry or necessarily been all that successful. There are possibly political reasons for this; for instance, the rest of the country prefers to think of Quebec as being only French-speaking. But so much of the history of poetry in Canada begins right here, in Quebec and Montreal in particular. Montreal remains the most cosmopolitan and cultural city in Canada. Culture here is a way of life, not an affectation or oddity as it sometimes seems to be in other parts of the country.

I have always found your work very strongly visual. Why do you think the visual is such a primary component in your poetry?

When I went to university I considered going into Fine Arts, instead I did something "practical" and went into Political Science and then, finally, English. When I was in high school I read Van Gogh's letters, and my cultural heroes were Van Gogh, Gauguin, Seurat, and the other Impressionists and Expressionists. My approach to writing poetry is fairly simple; I believe that the reader should be able to visualize what the poet writes as well as be moved emotionally by the poem. There also has to be a rhythm to the language; music is also very important to me. Despite my work reviewing poetry I really don't care if a poem is not a hundred percent well written. It has to move me emotionally. Well written poems that are merely intellectual, academic, or highly-crafted hold little interest for me. I have always taken photographs; since I was eleven or twelve years old I've had a camera. I used to pore over old family photographs;

this was part of my obsession with the past. I enjoy very much looking at books of photographs. In one of the poems in *The Trees of Unknowing* I mention Dostoyevsky's desk and that refers to a photograph of the writer's desk; just yesterday I came across a photograph of C.G. Jung's desk. So much of the inner self is revealed in his desk, just as Van Gogh revealed his inner self and the inner self of Gauguin in his two paintings of the chairs they used when they were together for a few months in Arles in the late 1880s. I am deeply moved by visual art, paintings, photographs, sculptures, water colours, drawings, and so on. I used to visit a friend in England every few years and I'd always visit the Tate Gallery to see the Rothkos, the marvelous paintings by William Turner, and the drawings by William Blake. When I visit Ottawa it's the National Gallery of Canada for the Group of Seven and the room of Henry Moore sculptures at the AGO in Toronto. So all of this is an important part of my work; writing and visual art don't exist in isolation from each other, they are part of the same creative process.

A lot of Canadian poetry is fairly emotionally restrained. In contrast, you don't seem to hold very much back in your poetry. Your work is highly personal and confessional. Can you explain this?

The answer to this lies in why I write poetry. I ask myself what is my main concern and since poetry is so important to me then obviously whatever I am urgently concerned with will find its place in my poetry. I remember reading in the late 60s something Allen Ginsberg said, "Scribble down your nakedness because it is the nakedness of the soul that people are really interested in reading about." I've had a lot to work out, to try to understand, in order to feel clear about myself and my life. Also, I had dreams when I was twelve years old that pretty much pushed me into writing about the things that I write about. These dreams were very direct statements to write about certain things that required greater clarity. Our society denies the importance of self-knowledge, denies our emotions, and so on; in comparison to the official attitude of our society, my work must seem unrestrained, although I don't think it is.

I don't like the term "confessional" poetry because it is not accurate; it doesn't properly describe the work of poets who have a need to take risks and live on an emotional and existential edge. We all have a dark side, what C.G. Jung termed the Shadow. Often my work explores inner darkness; this includes emotional pain, and obsession with the past and with death. In some ways I have crossed the line between the private and public person, because my work is basically all private. After I wrote the poem "Divisions," my writing changed—not really confessional because I have nothing to confess—but the barrier between the public and private person is gone. This doesn't mean divulging every private detail of one's life: only the essential parts that other people might find helpful in their lives, or the parts that fall into some kind of mythopoetic shaping of experience that is both personal and beyond personal. Basically all of my poetry is very moral and life affirming despite the solemnity of it, or a sometimes apparent bleakness. What I write about from my own life doesn't feel like it is just my personal property but belongs to whoever reads it, as long as I can fashion it, through art, into something that transcends the personal. Then the poetry has gone beyond the divisive and time imprisoned ego. I believe that poetry should take emotional risks; that it should not be afraid to go beyond emotional repression and fear—then it can have a psychically positive effect on the writer and the reader. It can help to wake us up; can help us to examine our lives.

Many poets reach a level of writing proficiency, where their writing is very good. In Canada we have that type of poet, people who write well, but they lack vision. I have reviewed almost a hundred poetry books over the last fifteen years and only a few show any evidence of the poet grappling with the essential things of life: how to live a decent life, how to be emotionally free, and the role of the spiritual in poetry. To write something and show technical skill in writing or originality in one's use of language—that's all very nice but if the poet isn't saying anything then it is all for nothing.

The real poet is capable of transcending our stereotyped ideas of what is important and to be valued in life. Poetry is the vehicle for this vision. This vision has to do with what Jung calls "individuation" and what others call self-knowledge and self-discovery, this must be one of the important purposes of life. But there is no formula to create this kind of great poet. This kind of writing, writing with vision, has to do with spirituality, with meaning, and with love.

***Divisions* is dedicated to your father and your son, and it always seemed to me to be a book that is very highly focused on the father-son relationship. In *Family Album* you seem to move out into the wider context of family and your place in it. The family extends in all directions, towards the past and towards the future while also dominating the present.**

Family has always been a concern of mine; for instance in 1971 I published, with another young poet, a chapbook called *Poems of a Period*. It contains poems about my grandmother and uncle; from when I began writing I have written about my family. When I began writing, consciously recording insights, poems, short stories, and my diary, I knew the family was my major preoccupation. My father came from a large family and my brother and I were the last children from among all the cousins, there was a considerable age gap between us and our other cousins, on the Morrissey side. I grew up attending a lot of funerals, surrounded by old people, with a sense of the transitoriness of life, and hearing the stories of my mother's childhood, and what life was like in the "good old days." I grieved for that lost time of innocence when everything seemed so much better than it was when I was a child. I also felt, when I was twelve and thirteen years old, that there was a quality of bravery about these people, that what they had done should be recorded for future generations or be lost. If I didn't record their experiences then no one would and they would be lost. Even in my own life, at that early age, I realized that I was forgetting things and I developed a mania for recording whatever I had done, for instance I started a diary when I went to the hospital to have my tonsils removed; this became a diary that I have kept everyday since I was fourteen years old. Also, writing has always been a way of making sense of my own life. I have a need for order and understanding; in writing about family and my own life I have come, I feel, to a greater understanding of my own life than I would otherwise have had. In fact, the writer mythologizes his or her life, turns experience into archetypes, turns the personal into the impersonal that is then available for whoever reads the work; and one hopes, that the reader will come away from one's work with a greater understanding of life. It can't all be just private, the writer must transcend the personal if the work is to last. That's part of the art of writing poetry. Apparently I chose to write about family, but I feel that the subject chose me: that, too, is the way writing works. My feeling is that writing about family came to me as a given subject and demanded to be put into words. The insights and choices of the twelve year old extend far into one's life...

Northrop Frye commented on the shiftings and interpenetrations of time and place in *Family Album*, and it is one of the book's most

distinctive features. Was that a conscious literary device you decided to employ, or did it just "happen" as you worked with the material?

I may be writing about one particular family, but at the same time my concern is with all families, and the repetition of experience throughout time. Many things are not under our conscious control: we think, as parents, that we shape our children, that they are blank slates when they are born. But with experience we see that the child is born substantially the way he or she will be later on in life, almost despite the way in which the child is treated. This is not to justify abuse of a child, but to say that how our children turn out, generous or selfish, loving or mean spirited, it isn't all under our control. We are basically modifications of whatever has preceded us, and whatever will eventually come is a modification of what we are today. In chronological time there are universal qualities, love, death, birth, youth, old age, being a mother or a father, and so on. These are all archetypal experiences. So the present, past, and future, and geography or place become one experience.

Finally, "the shifting and interpenetrations of time and place" was a conscious literary device; it is an effect that I wanted and the result of a lot of editing and years of work put into *Family Album* during a very stressful time in my life, a time when my writing was restrained because of the conflict in my first marriage. So those are poems that move toward the minimal, and they reflect how minimal and reduced I felt as a human being.

In earlier books like *The Trees of Unknowing* and *Divisions* your line breaks are often fragmented and fractured; this is especially true in *Divisions* where many of your images and statements have an almost shard-like quality. In *Family Album* there's more of a coherence as we move from line to line; the white spaces and silences aren't tugging at the words with the same kind of insistence. Do you think there's any reason for that change?

One matures as a writer, one's style develops, changes, it can't stay the same without exposing a lack of insight and development in one's life. Anyone who reads a lot of poetry has seen a young poet's first book, it seems brilliant, original, and has a quality of freshness; however, sometimes it lacks depth and maturity. In Canada we like brilliant first books by "poets," but we lack an audience for poetry that appreciates the more difficult and complex work that comes later in a poet's career. So, while *The Trees of Unknowing* was well received, *Divisions* is narrative and the rhythm of language is getting more complex; the themes and ideas are more complex as well. Many young poets stop writing, or they turn to writing prose poems or just plain prose. Poets who have done the work, make it a little easier for younger poets, they have persevered in their writing. Enough accolades are given to younger poets; we need to review fewer first books and pay more attention to what mature poets are saying. As poets age we have deeper insights into life and it seems fundamental that we should be listened to, assuming we really are getting more mature and not just repeating the style and themes of the past. I am committed to building a body of work that communicates something substantial enough that it interests the critics, but accessible enough that whoever reads my work will come away spiritually and emotionally moved. But this takes years of work, an entire lifetime, and in some ways I am only now beginning this major work of the second half of my life.

In your most recent book, *The Compass* , you continue to tackle the domain of the family, reaching back to ancestors, and reaching towards the future through your son. But you also write more about your status *within* the family.

Well, the family is no longer *out there*, but *in here*, it is no longer externalized; there is a greater understanding of the dynamics of the family. We grow older and understand better what our parents have gone through. We see that either they struggled and did their best, or they were weak and didn't protect or even love all that much when you most needed it, when you were a child. There is also a new authority that one gains with age; we are no longer the child who is at the mercy of adults' whims, but the adult ourselves. There is a new emotional, spiritual, and existential authority; I don't know if everyone has this experience but I can see it in my own life.

The second section of *The Compass* is called "Hades" for specific reasons. Divorce is a descent into hell; the family and home that took years to build is destroyed, in the time it takes to see your child drive away with your former mate. This is a devastating experience; but it has one redeeming aspect: it finally grows you up. So I get tired of hearing about men who are what Jung called "puer eternus"; these men, they are actually boys however old they are, can't really be trusted because their sensitivity has no basis in experience. Of course we want men to be sensitive to other people's feelings, but we also want it to come from an inner authority or else men (and women) can't really be trusted. So I would say that a person who has suffered, but not been crushed by his or her suffering, and who has gained an inner authority through the hard work of thinking deeply about life, this person writes from the center of his or her being and whatever is then written is from within experience, whether it is the family or what have you, and not from a distance, not from outside of experience.

In *The Compass* you also take on the question of renewing your own life. This book seems to be more about you, and your personal experiences.

This is certainly a book of self-discovery, the journey of self-discovery, as I have tried to make all of my books—works coming from a perception of the spiritual self. And it is a book of renewal, it begins with the family, with what is left of a once large family that has now dwindled to only a few people and the collective memories of the family. Then there is the "Hades" section that is concerned with divorce, separation, an elegy for what could have been but never was, and the devastation of suddenly losing everything and being alone. The final section, "The Compass," deals with finding a new love, and the experience of love; but it is still coming from me, they aren't really love poems, but poems of discovering love for the first time in my life; it is a tremendously powerful experience, an experience that is transformative and this is what the poems are saying: give all to love for love transforms and makes one whole.

When I look at the books I have written I can see a pattern forming. There was the early *The Trees of Unknowing* which was quite an innocent book, the language in it was celebratory and outgoing, it was a book of hope and longing and even of love; but it was also naive and lacking the depth that comes with age. This was followed by three other books that come from the depths of inner awareness, realizing that life is suffering, realizing that one is alone, self-conscious, unhappy; they are books from William Blake's spiritual category of Experience. *Divisions* dealt with my father's death and the feeling of being divided from society; the poems in *Family Album* are short, concise, all well written but highly controlled and they have lost the earlier exuberance for life. Finally, *The Compass* is a book about the descent into hell, there is no hope left but only to endure a limited vision of life and the self; even the final section where there is spiritual renewal through love and sexual union is a fairly ego-centric perception of experience. I think my work in progress, *The Yoni Rocks*, will be a book of higher innocence, of inner authority and vision. This new work returns to the exuberance and love of *The Trees of Unknowing* but goes beyond it. These are poems about love, sex, insight, but also elegies and an awareness of the transience of time. A chapbook of mine published in Edmonton, *The Divining Rod* is a book of love, sexuality and renewal. So these last two books, *The Yoni Rocks* and *The Divining Rod*, go together. We need a poetry that presents values and spiritual insight to a society that is destroying itself.

Back in the late seventies and early eighties you edited the *Montreal Journal of Poetics*. What were you trying to get done with that magazine?

First of all, the title of the magazine was a parody of academic periodicals, that part was a put-on, the rest was serious. I created this as a mail-out magazine that I photocopied, perhaps I mailed sixty copies of each issue to people I thought might be interested in receiving it. I never charged for it; I did it for the fun of doing it. I wanted to keep the publication dates irregular, that is, whenever I felt like putting out an issue I did. I published articles by many poets as well as my own articles; it was a place for me to publish ideas about poetry and poetics. I kept it going from 1978 to 1985, when I felt it was time to move on to other things.

You've done a lot of reviewing of Canadian poetry books; how do you feel about what's going on in contemporary Canadian poetry?

I have reviewed books by unknown writers to the few real poets that we have in this country. On the whole I am fairly optimistic about Canadian poetry. At any time in a country's history to have two or three real poets is an achievement, and we have several first rate world class poets. Then there are the many people who write poetry as a pastime, who aren't really poets but who enjoy having one or possibly two books of their verse published, and there is a place for this in a national literature as well. Many poetry books couldn't have been published without the Canada Council and this has both a positive and negative side to it; the writers can only do their part in this job of creating a national culture, then it is also up to schools and the individual's own desire to be both an educated and cultured person. Of course the final critic of art is time, and most contemporary poetry will be forgotten; but that is true for literature of any country in the world. Culture, art, poetry, music, this is what saves us as a society from being submerged by popular culture; the collective heritage of culture going back thousands of years is what connects us to something beyond the currently fashionable; art, poetry, culture, this is what saves this age from materialism.

How does it feel to be an Anglo author in Quebec these days? Do you think things have changed since the early 7Os, when you started as a writer?

The English speaking writer in Quebec has been a part of a living culture; being a writer may have seemed eccentric in other parts of the country, but writing has always been a possibility for young writers here; it wasn't viewed as something bizarre, eccentric. Layton, Dudek, Scott were all familiar names to me while I was in high school in Montreal; some even lived in my neighbourhood and we read their poems in our school anthologies. Meanwhile, Hugh MacLennan lived and wrote about life in Montreal and every young person read *Two Solitudes* in school. This was all very exciting for a young person who wanted to write, as these older writers provided inspiration and were models for the writer's life. Modern Canadian literature began in Montreal; if you wanted to be a writer in Canada you lived for a while in Montreal.

But this has proved to be a fool's paradise: a wealthy and therefore powerful minority has little place in a modern democracy; inevitably, the English in Montreal have moved west, some for political reasons, others for economic gain. Quebec has changed radically in the last twenty-five years; it is clearly a French speaking province now. We were a happy but closed community and I regret that our numbers have diminished as they have. I like being an English-speaking Quebecker and I am proud of our history and the achievements of our community.

June 16, 1991-December 17, 1992

Stephen Morrissey and Ken Norris, 1990.

Islands, Politics & the Persistence of Poetry
An Interview with Ken Norris

Sonja Skarstedt, *Zymergy* 7, Spring 1990

As the author of over fifteen collections of verse, it would appear that you are a rather prolific writer—and some say that a prolific output doesn't necessarily mean a qualitative output. Agree?

No, or mostly no. I don't think a writer's being painstakingly cautious is any guarantee of "quality"; often it's just a sign of playing it safe. I like writers who take risks, and often they are shamelessly prolific: D.H. Lawrence and Melville; in Canada Layton, Dudek, Souster, Bowering, McFadden. There aren't too many writers who remain prolific throughout an entire career. Most of us slow down at some point. But why not be prolific when you're young; you've got a lot of energy then. Writing is a new tool, a new power, and anyone with curiosity will try to explore the possibilities for writing as much as possible. If you're living in a creative environment to boot, you're sparking off things all the time. That's certainly what was happening for me in my first decade as a published writer. When I was younger I was writing all the time. I don't do that anymore; now I enjoy the freedom of not having to write.

What about the amount of time it takes to work up a manuscript?

In 1985 I published a book, *One Night*, that I wrote in an afternoon. But then the new book I've got coming out with Quarry, *In the House of No*, has taken me five years to complete. An early book, *The Perfect Accident*, also had about five years behind it. So I understand the necessity of taking five years to complete a book, but I also understand the experience of writing them really fast. Most of my books have taken a couple of years.

What prompted you to travel in the North and South Pacific?

I guess I was aware of completing a particular life cycle and I was looking for something new, something different. I'd lived in cities all my life, and I wanted to try living in a garden. A lot of things were ending—an important relationship, school, the whole experiment at Véhicule—and I just wanted to find a new inspiration, a new way of life. Once I went there I got hooked, so I kept going back.

How long did it take you to "settle in" to life in the Pacific?

I don't think I ever settled in. It was important that it remain exotic.

Whenever it started to feel familiar I'd usually start thinking about heading back to North America. The sense of "otherness" was very important to me. At the same time, I certainly internalized a lot of that experience, in an attempt to find some kind of internal wholeness. It fed me, and in certain ways it healed me. I was able to put a certain kind of desperation I felt in my twenties to rest. It made the world seem to me like a far less hostile place. It gentled my soul.

Did you go to the Pacific with the intention of writing *The Better Part of Heaven* and later, *Islands*?

I went with my heart and my notebook open. Things were happening and I had to write about them. I was keeping a journal that turned into a book. All of the structuring of *The Better Part of Heaven* was worked out later with bpNichol as we edited the book. I was just journal-keeping, every now and then realizing I'd written a pretty good poem. On the other hand, *Islands* was produced much more self-consciously. When I did the first trip I just spent my mad money and flew off into the unknown. For *Islands* I'd gotten a Canada Council grant and knew I was going off to write another book. *The Better Part of Heaven* had established to me how to structure *Islands*. The next time I went back I rejected that structure and worked with the form of the open meditative long poem; that produced "The Wheel," which is Book Ten of *Report*. My last time back, in 1988, I went back to writing short poems and prose narrative. So each trip has, happily, yielded a book.

Ken Norris in Fiji, 1985.

Did you originally intend that *The Better Part of Heaven* would be an integral part of *Report on the Second Half of the Twentieth Century*?

I've never been big on pre-planning. At a certain point after the work is written it becomes clear to me what it means and where it belongs. In Book 4 of *Report* I'd flown out to the West Coast, looked out over the Pacific, and then flown home. It seemed obvious to me that *The Better Part of Heaven* was the next step.

Did living in the Pacific widen the scope of *Report*? If so, how?

It got me out of my little artistic enclave in Montreal. It showed me another world that existed as part of the world. I flew half a world away, away from everything I knew, and let the impact of that change in location register. It let me escape from the gravitational pull of North America and Europe for a while. From the South Seas I began to see the Far East. It shifted the centre and let me out of the box I was in the process of creating for myself.

Was the Pacific paradisal, an ambrosia for hyper-techno-burnout?

It was paradise and it wasn't paradise. It was beautiful and it wasn't perfect, except insofar as it was. Sometimes it was far from perfect, as in Truk or in the Marshall Islands. Not just for me, I mean, but for the people living there. And overall, I rarely met *anyone* who thought they were living in paradise. The locals were just living their lives. On Bora Bora, which is the most beautiful place I've ever seen, the teenagers were bored shitless and couldn't wait till they could move to Papeete, the "big city" in Tahiti, or, better yet to go to Los Angeles! For them it was like living in small-town Canada, and many of them wanted to go off and "see the world." Get away from coconuts, taro and fish: to have a Big Mac, fries and a Coke. Whatever's different is what's exotic.

There's a sense of connectedness, travel, continuity in these poems. Has Louis Dudek's concept of the "travelling poem" influenced you?

Well, Louis covered the Atlantic and I covered the Pacific. There's an influence there, sure. "The Wheel" probably has the most in common with long poems like "Atlantis" and "Continuation." Both *The Better Part of Heaven* and *Islands* are books that are comprised of individual pieces that narrate a story. I find that an interesting formal device, and I suppose it's rooted in various ideas about the long poem. It's linked lyrics with prose islands. I suppose the biggest influence for this form would be Basho and Issa.

Neruda's poetry seems to have had a big influence, playing a role in the nurturing/development of your own voice. True?

Very true. I've been deeply influenced by his poetry since I was seventeen. Ten or so of my poems are "translations" of Neruda; perhaps more correctly I should call them appropriations or adaptations of Neruda. That was something I learned to do more wholeheartedly from (Peter) van Toorn. In the beginning I was a very cautious translator of Neruda; now I try to incorporate him into my poetic voice. I think he serves as my link to Whitman, though he is, of course, a very powerful poet in his own right. His work helped me to locate my own political voice.

Do poetry and politics mix? Especially in "apolitical" Canada?

It seems to me that it is *essential* that poetry have a political dimension, *especially* in a country like Canada. Poetry is political. Anything that works against silence and complacency has political energy. Can you separate politics out of life? I don't think so. I don't think that you can put politics and art into two separate camps either.

I was lamenting the relative uselessness of poetry in Canada when I met Elias Letelier-Ruz. Here was a Chilean exile who had been imprisoned and tortured for writing poetry. I had no choice but to help him translate his poems into English; I felt like I had to enable him to "get the word out" in English. I felt I owed it to him, I owed it to the spirit of Neruda, I owed it to myself, and I owed it to my country. In the process of translating his work I became much more politicized than I had been. After all, what politics are all about is morality. It's not a question of who's in, who's out, of voting for Mulroney, Turner or Broadbent; it's a question of justice and human dignity. As far as I'm concerned, any poetry that is not concerned with this is worthless.

Does your work stem more from a private vision, than from dealing directly/indirectly with politics? Or a mixture of both?

I remember seeing this old TV clip of Pierre Berton interviewing Leonard Cohen. Cohen said something about how the first thing he does when he wakes up in the morning is try to determine whether he's in a state of grace. For most people in the world that would be an extremely luxurious position. We live isolated in a society that is materially prosperous and relatively unhampered when it comes to questions of individual freedoms. I say relatively unhampered; for instance, I live in the U.S. now and the Supreme Court recently made several rulings on abortion that, in effect, put American women in the position of being second-class citizens. Can you really separate out private vision and social interface? I don't think so. What are private visions *about?* Sometimes they're just about personal psycho-babble, but usually they have some kind of social correlative. I can't help but be aware of the fact that, if I were Chilean or Somalian, or a black South African, I could be waking up each morning in a prison cell. I don't but others do. That increasingly has an impact upon my writing.

When I was younger all I knew was I wanted to be a writer. Why? I suppose there was some process of self-aggrandizement going on. There are people you want to prove your worth to. But once you become a writer, what do you do? What did I want to write about? After you've been writing for a while your subject matter finds you. If I write about myself now it's as a "sample" life; it could be anybody's. But if being able to write is empowering, then it seems to me really senseless to squander the power that words have. So that any helpful change I can make using words seems worthwhile to me, whether it's writing a poem or writing a letter to a foreign government.

You mentioned Neruda earlier...do you have any other "influences"?

You're talking about literary influences, and I can, of course, rattle off a list of authors as long as my arm. But music has been a big influence, Robert Johnson and Billie Holiday. Eric Clapton is a great musical phrasemaker, and he plays in my head a lot of the time when I'm writing. Right now I'm entranced by Bach and Vivaldi. As far as poetry goes, Artie Gold and bpNichol and bill bissett are poets who really affected me when I was a bit younger and a lot more impressionable. I have great respect for Canadian poets like Scott and Klein, the Cerberus group, Leonard Cohen and Phyllis Webb. And I like the Japanese poets Basho and Issa a lot. American poets Frank O'Hara, William Bronk, and Stephen Rodefer have all opened aesthetic doors for me. Lately I'd say that Wordsworth has been registering major impact.

Are you interested in branching into prose, plays, essays?

I've occasionally tried my hand at prose fiction; I've got two bad novels buried in the bottom drawer. I started out wanting to be a novelist. I wanted to be the new F. Scott Fitzgerald. But then I kept thinking about how his life didn't turn out so great. Ultimately, I find that I get bored when I'm writing fiction, so I don't think it's really my medium. A number of people pointed out to me that I was telling stories in the Pacific books, but they were like a page long. All the set-up time in fiction really doesn't interest me. Drama actually interests me more. Tennessee Williams is a writer whose work I really admire. If I was going to do playwriting I'd probably try to write stuff like *Sweet Bird of Youth* or *Night of the Iguana*, or that other Southern play *Crimes of the Heart*, plays with really off-beat characters. I've got no interest in writing fiction or drama that glorifies middle class life, or even attempts to be a slice of it. As for essays: being an academic requires them, but they're all scholarly-based.

I note that you had a hand in various projects, anthologies and so forth. Do you enjoy the role of editing?

Nah, I hate it. It's just that I keep getting these great ideas for anthologies. And I seem to be someone who is willing to do all the shit work one needs to do in order to get an anthology into print.

What are some of the pitfalls of being an editor, then?

It's a great way to make enemies. No one *ever* thanks you for including them in an anthology. That's because they believe that they deserve to be included in every anthology ever to be published. A lot of people get angry about being left out. Some get snarky about what work of theirs you choose to include. So editing an anthology is disastrous for your social life.

Are there any benefits?

Knowing you've done a good job. An occasional royalty cheque for thirty-seven dollars. When I was a kid I was a compulsive list-maker. I used to write down the top forty songs every week from about 1960 to 1965. Some of that kind of energy goes into my anthologizing. I suppose one can make the argument that anthologies influence literary taste. I like being able to spotlight the work of writers I respect, and to give attention to people who have been overlooked. *Canadian Poetry Now* has an equal number of men and women; I think that's important.

How do you go about the task of writing at this point in your life? Do you have any sort of schedule?

For the past couple of years I've been mostly editing work that's already been written. I have never kept banker's hours when it comes to writing; I don't have any kind of schedule. I write everything down in notebooks, tidy it up later on typewriter or computer. I pay a lot of attention to my selection of notebooks and pens. Right now I've got five notebooks filled with work that will eventually have to be dug out of the notebooks and put into some kind of shape. I tend to cut rather than rewrite. I very rarely change the overall structure of a piece. I never write a poem from an idea I've had. Poetry is an improvisational art for me. I start out in a key and see what I can work towards.

You've been living in the U.S. since 1985. Any feeling of exile?

At first. From time to time. I moved to the States to take up a teaching job at the University of Maine, teaching Canadian literature. Before I moved down I took out Canadian citizenship, after being a landed immigrant for about a decade.

These days I think of myself as inhabiting the margin. Maine really is a kind of no-man's land between the U.S. and Canada. Where I live now (Bangor, Maine) is somewhat slightly north of Montreal. Certainly it's farther north than Toronto. So the landscape is very similar, even if the governmental machinery is American. As (George) Bowering noted somewhere, I'm CanLit's New England representative. I'm getting the word out on CanLit stateside. When I teach Canadian Literature I teach it as a foreign literature. I've taken out a lot of magazine subscriptions, and the Double Hook (Book Store, Montreal) sends down boxes full of new releases. My daughter lives out in the Eastern Townships, so I'm actually up in Quebec quite regularly.

I figure I'm kind of in a similar position to the one Robert Kroetsch was in back in the late sixties—he was teaching at SUNY-Binghamton for about seventeen years before heading up to Manitoba. If I eventually move back up to Canada then Kroetsch can serve as my model. If not, then it's A.J.M. Smith, who taught at Michigan State for something like thirty-five years. In academia you have to be willing to go where the work is. The University of Maine has the biggest Canadian Studies program in the U.S., so I figure it's an interesting place to be.

You spent quite a chunk of your life here in Montreal. What was it about those years...that made them "magical"?

There were a lot of things going on. It was a great time to be a young writer, bringing out my first books. It was great to be a young editor at Véhicule, helping to put together books by other young writers whose work excited me. Artie Gold and I virtually lived at each other's houses around 1978-79; we were together a lot of the time, and Artie was someone whose work I really respected and whose friendship I really treasured. The whole Véhicule experiment was in full swing, and all of that activity taught me that the poet is not an isolato, that writing is a communal act. All of the Vehicule poets were deep inside each other's work. It was very intense, very joyous. I worked with (Endre) Farkas on the Montreal anthology, and with van Toorn a short time later on *Cross/cut*. Sometimes being a Vehicule Poet was like being in a great rock band; at least that's the way I remember it. The highs were really high, and the lows were pretty ephemeral. We knew we were changing the history of Canadian poetry forever. The change has been maybe more subtle than perhaps we'd hoped for, but I think it's there. And certainly that association changed the lives of all of us.

Were the Vehicule Poets doing something different than, say, what was happening in Montreal in the Sixties?

I may be wrong, but it always seemed to me that not very much was going on in Montreal in the late sixties. The early sixties appear to have been somewhat more interesting. But, simply, the action had shifted to other places; the new innovations were no longer coming into Canada via Montreal anymore. The Véhicule crowd was very interested in the New York School, the Beats, the San Francisco poets, as well as the *Tish* and Coach House crowds. And we were very dedicated to getting things done. We ran readings, published books, made videotapes, and got poetry onto the city buses.

Is there such a thing as "literature" anymore? Or has the existence of the Canada Council turned art into "open season" for hustlers?

I teach literature; I teach Shakespeare and Melville, Wordsworth and Blake. I also teach the occasional course in contemporary Canadian writing. I like the word "writing." I don't like being in a position where I have to confer the status of "literature" upon a piece of contemporary writing. I'm not big on devising hierarchies.

That's a bit of an aside to your question, maybe. There are hustlers in business and there are hustlers in the arts. There are a lot of people who want something for nothing, and there are a lot of people who say that they want to be writers when what they really want is to be famous. I don't think that the Canada Council has "ruined" the arts in Canada. I don't believe in the virtues of capitalism enough to agree with John Metcalf that the marketplace should be the testing ground for literary excellence. I know excellent writers who have never received a Canada Council grant, and I know of untalented people who are very good at writing grant proposals. What matters is the work. Very little of what's being published right now will be read two hundred years from now. It's unfortunate that very little of what's being published right now is being read right now.

One of Louis Dudek's more notorious statements with regard to poetry is: "It's a mug's game." How would you interpret this?

If you write poetry expecting recognition you're bound to be disappointed. Being a poet in the twentieth century North American society is just about the stupidest thing you can do with your life. There are few material rewards. There are few spiritual rewards. If you have a choice, do something else. If you don't have a choice, try to do the best that you can.

What does an author do in the absence of an audience?

He or she persists. A.M. Klein didn't call his poem "Portrait of the Poet as Nobody" just out of thin air; he was responding to something he felt very deeply: that there was no place for him in the modern world, no role to fulfill. He changed the title, but the poem talks about his feeling like a convict on parole, about his feelings of almost total obscurity. I can relate to that very easily. Popular culture is flashy and shallow, and you find it everywhere, even in the Cook Islands. I was on the isolated French Polynesian island of Maupiti a few years back, and *Fraggle Rock* came on the TV at the hotel where I was staying! It blew my mind at the time, but it shouldn't have. The communications network blankets the world pretty thoroughly. The event would have been if I'd found a copy of a Canadian poetry book there, which I didn't.

The audience for CanLit is very small. Someone publishing a book with McClelland and Stewart might have three times the readers I have, but that's maybe a thousand people. In his essay on failure in the second *MacMillan Anthology*, Dudek tells us that the young writer should prepare for failure, not success. I think that's essentially true.

You once mentioned something about "paying your dues" via publishing when you were in your twenties—and that now it's time for your generation to "get on" with its own writing while the next does its share of production-work... Elaborate?

I think your question misinterprets what I was saying. You make it sound like I think that the younger generation should be lackeys while the older poets reap all of the rewards. What I was saying is that I think younger writers should be willing to take over the means of production, by starting a reading series, a press, a magazine like *Zymergy*. I really don't see all of the work I did with Véhicule and CrossCountry Press as "paying my dues." That was all really fun time. And I think being involved in those enterprises helped me to get taken seriously as a writer. I more or less self-published my first few books; those that didn't come out with Véhicule came out with CrossCountry. I started publishing in 1975; by 1979 the editors at Coach House, the press I just *idolized* as a young writer, were asking to see my next manuscript. Michael Ondaatje passed on a couple of them before bpNichol decided to edit *The Better Part of Heaven*. But rather than sitting on my first book for 5 or 6 years I decided to just get work *out*. Getting the work out made me visible, made me *exist* as a writer.

Also, running Véhicule gave us power base, gave us some clout. I hate it when I see young poets who want to be discovered; it's just so passive. Most of us aren't brilliant writers at twenty-five, and most literary editors don't find themselves going "Eureka! A full-blown genius!" too often when reading manuscripts. Rather than being brilliant in our living rooms, the Véhicule crowd was willing to be not-so-great at public reading. But we learned so much by making those public mistakes. We grew up in public. I still love those early books, though I'm happily willing to admit that the only one of us who really had his act together back then was Artie.

I have a great respect for writers like Ondaatje and Frank Davey who are still involved in publishing young writers. I try to help Endre out with The Muses' Company. I think young writers should get involved; I think they should devote their lives to making literature *happen*. And I think you do that by taking hold of some aspect of the means of production.

What about the respect factor?

I think respect is always earned. But I think there's a reason why most cultures teach a respect for the older and wiser, and that's because there is a certain amount of wisdom that comes with age. We learn through experience.

There's nothing quite like the arrogance of the young; it is totally uninformed and totally sure of itself. Scott and Smith went about bumping off the Confederation poets for writing crappy poetry before they'd ever read them. This kind of thing happens all the time. The *Tish* poets said insulting things about older Montreal poets they had never bothered to read. I am sure that there are a number of young poets who, were I standing on a ledge, would have no compunction about pushing me off. They'd simply be getting rid of another older poet who was standing in their way.

I was a young poet once too, so I know. I remember when van Toorn and I were working on putting together the *Cross/cut* anthology; we'd sent away for permission rights to use some of Layton's poetry, and McClelland and Stewart was asking for a lot of money, money that just wasn't available to us. We were sitting around Peter's house, wondering how we were going to deal with this situation. I think I should add that Peter was very devoted to Layton's poetry at the time; he'd been working on an anthology of the greatest Canadian poems, and like a sixth of the book was Layton, forty poems or something. I wasn't quite as impressed. Anyway, Peter's saying "What are we going to do? How are we going to deal with this?" I was feeling frustrated, and I'd just seen the movie *His Girl Friday*, so I said "Why don't we just tell him that his poetry is lousy and kick him down the stairs?" I don't think I've ever seen anybody so shocked in my entire life! Van Toorn just looked at me aghast, like I'd disemboweled a sheep in the living room or something. But *that's* the arrogance of youth, that attitude, that willingness to be totally dismissive. I would never *think* of saying something like that about *any* poet these days; my appreciation of the struggle has deepened. And I would certainly never say it about Layton, whose effort to establish a place for poetry in this society should be honored. I now know that poetry didn't begin and doesn't end with me. When I was younger I could delude myself into believing it did.

Where do you think you are in your own career?

I think I'm in the middle of it. Psychologically I'm getting ready to put together a first selected poems and to get into what that means. The first stage of my writing life is over. As William Carlos Williams says in "The Desert Music," "I am a poet!" I know this to be true. I've done some good work, more than I really anticipated doing by this point in my life. I always figured I'd get good after forty-five, that the first twenty years or so would just be a long apprenticeship. Of course it has been and it is, but I feel that I've written some good poems along the way. I'm at the point of consolidating what I've done up until this point, before going on to the next big change.

You've always promoted "experimental" writing, yet your own work doesn't seem all that experimental. How do you account for this?

Probably my favorite sentence from all the reviews written about my work is this one: "Ken Norris' poetry is deceptive." W.J. Keith wrote that in a review of *Eight Odes*. He goes on to say that a second reading of that book totally changed his mind about what he thought I was doing. I think a lot of people have read my work *once*, and figure I'm kind of this generation's Raymond Souster. Simple, accessible, goes down easy, like lite beer. That isn't my work (nor Souster's). With a few exceptions I think most have missed the boat entirely. Artie and I were the two most ostensibly conservative Vehicule Poets. I'm still always willing to play straight man for Tom (Konyves) any time he wants to do a rewrite of the Marx Brothers. I suppose I feel a bit like Bowering in the *Tish* crowd and Ondaatje in the Coach House crowd: the seeming straight. But there's a lot going on in my work that no one has ever touched upon.

What kind of plans do you have for the future?

I've got a few books planned. A new one with Quarry due out this spring. Another installment of the *Report* sequence soon. An eventual selected. I intend to keep publishing parts of *Report* throughout the decade, and to do a collection of poems every four or five years. I plan to *improve*, that's my biggest plan.

Some say there are too many poets in Canada. What do you think?

Those who say there are too many poets are concerned with their own sales and their own reputations. When we were the Vehicule Poets we were the too many poets in the eyes of the slightly older generation. Now that we've been around for a while they seem to have gotten used to us. At the time they were afraid of us stealing their thunder, which we did whenever we could. But to say that there are too many poets is like saying that there are too many flowers, that there is too much truth, too much light. I just don't think so. Every good poem is a radiant message to the world, and I would be thrilled if every person in the world was busy working on poems. You couldn't give them all Canada Council grants, which is what troubles some people. But poetry isn't about money and glory and fame; it's a revelation of life, of living, of joy, of exuberance. And there can never be too much of that!

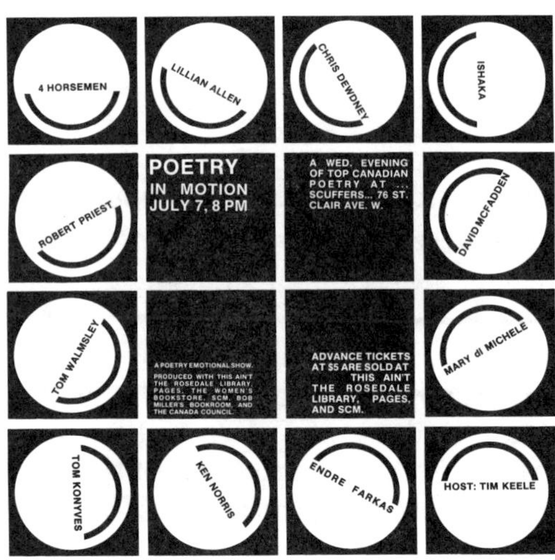

Ashes

Claudia Lapp

I scatter these chips, rough, brittle, dry,
into the shallow, melodious stream,
its bank winter brown, its trees in sap fullness.
Crow caws, a woodpecker tapping his tune
and unknown birdsongs assemble
for this ceremony of closure.
The ashes hit the air as mica flakes,
sink into stream bed as gold dust,
substance of my father's body returned to earth.

My hands are dry and grey with ash,
its grit pushes under my nails.
In this sacred time,
the world stands still enough for me
to feel its true rhythms and airs.
In a mild sky, the clouds move, gossamer and slow,
and at the moment of release,
ash glinting in sunlight,
a hawk circles above again and again.

2/21/87

In the Dark

Claudia Lapp

When the guide switched off the light
so we could experience the true darkness of
        this burial chamber deep in the green hills of County Meath,
so we could feel how *they* felt the dark,
5,000 years ago or so,
we were standing almost touching,
you so near I could feel the electricity
coming off your hair and wool shoulders
and I wanted her to keep that light off
so we could move closer, till touching,
the darkness could cover my arms flying about you,
releasing us from the charged restraint
we'd been maintaining since our eyes met.
Into this tomb/womb built by those who
  honoured the solstices we filed,
to brush up against a past mostly obscure,
and found our reaching senses amplified
in the chamber of stones so skillfully piled
to house the ashes of the dead.

Never were we closer than in that ancient dark.

7/13/88

Darning the World

Claudia Lapp

Opening my mother's sewing box,
of inlaid wood, from Germany,
makes me infinitely sad.
It happens each time:
the small familiar tools,
the same ones she handled,
speak of her in thimble and thread language
in accents of wartime wartime wartime,
lost buttons, torn hems, severed arms.

And tonight is the night.
The sock will be darned.
The proper needle, the correct thread color
        falls into my nimble hands.
It goes well for once, the darning.
The hole yields to surgery, closes stitch by stitch,
smoothly, without a lump to cause discomfort.
Does my mother's spirit preside?
It makes me infinitely sad,
for in that sewing box nestle all women,
darning, tending the small mendings for daughters,
for sons, for mates they're missing, for those
who've been missed and will be missed and missing forever
the world over and over again and darning still, in peace
and war and peace repairing the world, pulling it together,
thread by thread, re-piecing it, with love and devotion.

Full moon, 12/1/90

Family

Endre Farkas

Squiggles,
bits and pieces of this and that
and something else
rhythmically, magically, get us there.

From diapers to death
total chaos and confusion
are the politics of family.

From breakfast to suppers
to leftovers, lives gather dust
under beds never made.

So much noise
Circuits go
Wires short.

Children drop in, drop out
are remembered at odd moments
while comparing the price of eggs.

We grow up
are put in charge
become the parents of parents.

But there is a child somewhere
hiding from the storm
yearning for something.

Too tired for late-night walks
to stare at stars, to reach inside
to touch flesh

Something real says
gather up all the toys
for tomorrow comes early
and stays all day

August/93

Fathers & Sons

for my father
Endre Farkas

Your fingertips make a temple roof over me.
Your eyes close; shut out the horror.
Your lips murmur chants against the enslaving world.

Before the ritual of the first holy meal
As prescribed by ancient laws
A benediction.

Quiet tears follow;
Flow down your cheeks.
They bless
They plead
I taste them.

I am the prodigal son;
A ghost messiah that haunts desire
And each new year
Returns to be locked in your loving embrace.

All sons are lost.
All fathers fail.
Exilcd from each other,
We do not speak of flight.
We pretend that all is right.

May 27/92

Jazzing

Endre Farkas

Soft saxophone-rain rains on the jazzy pavement
Shines up the leaves on the way down
Slips its notes in and out of summer windows
In and out of dreams of who knows who
Counterpoints the moon's clarinet light
Wedged in fedora clouds.
And the distant train's horn sounds the coming
Driving rhythm right through the misty mood
Zinging along glistening tracks
And is gone, gone, gone
Leaving soft sad silence under foggy lights
Listening to the shimmering.
Feeling so sad/so good
Awake so late/so lost in the stars.

June 11/92

The Whip

Stephen Morrissey

1
Grandfather's cat 'o nine tails
kept in his dresser drawer
was enough to keep Mother in fear.
In her old age, knitting by the
television, the memory of the whip returned.
When my father died I retreated
inside myself, a socially acceptable
autistic who could hardly navigate between rooms
without getting lost or absorbed for hours
in the pattern of floor tiles;
I holed up in daydreams
and stared into space on the edge
of Hades, spinning in a vertigo
of fears. The next time I felt like
fainting was thirty-five years later when my wife
announced she was "unhappy with our
marriage"; "What's new?" I mentally replied
having been jettisoned from her affection
years before; our marriage was an alliance
of secrets and hopes that the other
might not notice the grimace we wore.
It was only weeks after the wedding
that we quarreled and she threw her ring
spinning end on end in space across the room
then rolling beneath a radiator
to rest in the previous year's dust;
I snatched up the ring and wanted to swallow it,
seeing how it became a snake curled
ready to strike; she had invaded my life
and since she had over two hundred
personalities I never knew who she'd be:
one day Mother Teresa, the next
the bride of Frankenstein bellowing
for quiet before she must
let the monster lie between
her legs. I disappeared inside myself
collecting rare books,
photographs of desks used by famous
people, and a radio still

receiving 1950s radio dramas
we listened to at 9 pm every night
as children, before being lulled to sleep
by darkness and prayers.

2
Grandfather's whip could dance across
the floor like the wizard-apprentice's
broom that came uncontrolled to life; the whip
seemed to fly through the air as if in orgy
of flagellation—the imagined pain
was pleasurable to us
for we hated our lives and would quickly
destroy whatever we built, for it was always
us and it was never good enough. Now
let the whips of the past lash out,
it is a tongue embedded in your ear.
We become invisible, lost in shadows
of who we are, and when I'm alone
I fold up and enter
suspended animation
until revived by voices
approaching the house, unhook myself
from the back of a closet door
and come to life. In the pattern of curtains
or clouds, faces emerge
so closely resembling your own
that you might reach up and touch
your cheek, neck, lips, move your
hand through your own hair as though
it belonged to someone else
you would be willing to touch
and offer at last a facsimile
of affection.

3
Grandfather was a fireman
and so I've grown up lighting
a few fires for the full effect
of communion with him.
He lived alone his last dozen years
until he transmuted into a sick
old man. He once slapped

my face, a twelve year old
too afraid to fight back.
Perhaps he was still angry
from when I set his house on fire, age eight,
dropping lit matches in the mail box
until curtains burst into flames;
by then his cat 'o nine tails
had long since disappeared,
in my imagination it still whipped our backs
and arms. Years later
his face returns,
enveloped in cigarette smoke
and anger, surfacing from the depths
of forgetfulness.

The Clothes of the Dead

Stephen Morrissey

I have worn the clothes of the dead
a second cousin's sweater,
already old when he died, I wore it
another dozen years;
my stepfather's scarves—
blue wool from Scotland,
white silk, and a yellow
Viella shirt. These were their
second skins I pulled on
inhabiting the shape of their
old clothes for years before
the clothes wore out;
days governed by clothes
unfolded and worn,
then thrown into a laundry hamper
or balled and kicked across
the floor. Now those clothes
are gone—eaten by moths,
torn into holes and rips
not even good as rags. I wore
my own clothes
like the clothes of the dead:
brown corduroy trousers, a sweater
shapeless and small even when new;
I pulled it over my head and assumed
the facial expressions of an old man—
these clothes aged me
into someone twice my age
sexless and afraid of life thinking
of retirement and paying off a mortgage;
the penalty of a marriage of lies
held together by threads,
thread-bare of love
a wardrobe
of secrets and despair.
Today I burned six shirts,
two sweaters and trousers:
I burn the past out of my
life, return to living
from dying, take what

I have been,
clothes that made me
someone I didn't want to be
or someone I was but never liked,
clothes that are days and months and years
of a life I gave up
to fear and despair.
Now those clothes are gone:
        ashes of clothes
        ashes of former selves
        ashes of time and space
        ashes of words and notebooks
        ashes of thoughts
                and flesh and blood
        ashes of one who surrendered

The Road to Soufriere

Ken Norris

What can one say about the road to Soufriere?

That it is under repair
and when it is fixed it still won't be worth shit.

That it takes two full hours
of driving on the left side of the road
to cover the 28 miles from Castries.

That once down in the valley
and after a rain
you will slide along the rim of banana plantations
travelling mud-deep roads.

That, arriving, in Anse La Raye,
you are likely to be misdirected
by some friendly townspeople
and you will drive helplessly
along streets lined with tin shacks
before finding the right road again,
passing over a sheet metal bridge
you are convinced will collapse at any moment.

That for miles between Anse La Raye and Canaries
you will be enraptured by the sublime.

That you will honk your horn
going around a thousand blind turns.

That the farmers
who appear out of nowhere
will all be carrying machetes.

That the descent into Canaries
will fill you with tenderness
for the children in their blue school uniforms,
and the ascent out of Canaries
along a road surrounded on both sides by steep drops
will have you praying for your life.

That in the middle of absolute nowhere
three men will stop your car
and try to sell you coconuts.

That you will nervously decline.

That the beautiful and the sublime
will flow into and out of one another like lovers
and you will make voodoo sacrifices
to the safety of your tires.

That four miles outside of Soufriere
you will be stopped by another three men
claiming to be government agents
who will insist that you take one of them for your tour guide
in order to protect you from the harassment and harm
they themselves are.

That you will be instructed
to take a scenic photograph of the distant Pitons
by the ostensible tour guide you don't want.

That you will scare your tour guide shitless
by almost driving off the road
where there is nothing but vertical drop
because his presence is making you nervous.

That, on the outskirts of Soufriere,
your tour guide will ask to be let out of the car
before you ever get a chance to check his bogus credentials
at the St. Lucian Tourist Bureau.

That, at long last, you will arrive in Soufriere
where many other St. Lucians
will try and stop your car
and aggressively demand to be your tour guide.

That you will be surprised
by how forcefully you say no.

That the Pitons will stand
majestically and impassively
the whole time above the human equation.

That after finding a quiet place
to compose yourself and have lunch,
and after a somewhat closer look at the Pitons
or maybe a trip to the Volcano

you will have to drive the whole way back again.

Without question, you will make it.

St. Lucia

The Night

Ken Norris

The music I find
in an old forgotten book
is rare enough, rich enough
to enable me to make a purchase upon the stars.

The night is long
and I am sleepless,
restless with the condition
of having too much, and wanting everything.

Into This Space

Tom Konyves

light at first penetrates uneasily in long pencil-thin strokes, unsettling dust before moving on, ever upward, bouncing from glass to metal in Pan-like strides yet without any semblance of mischief or grace. Its touch is warm, it's true, yet it pretends not comfort or joy. Impossible to deduce a will moving invisible yet causing enlightenment. At mid-day, the creator walks into the path of light streaming through the crusted window and interrupts the silence with a song. The beams know it not, nor the nocturnal roaches and the mirror is blind, the dust unforgiving.

Into this space

water drips mysteriously, avoiding the snare of a patient tin can with its random bursts. The roof was coated in all the likely places, yet the uneven tap of water persists, a benefit for an unknown tree in an impenetrable forest.

Into this space

two lovers have escaped to spend an uninterrupted night together. The calm of the neighbourhood does not diminish their fear of discovery. They nearly trip upon a cot, over which he spreads his long black coat, then sits to remove his boots. She is cold under the cover, sitting and hugging her knees, and rocking, attempting to see through the dark. His whispers grow more urgent, yet she moves not, and is silent. He laughs into the silence, to which she replies with a whisper, then a kiss, and a touch.

Into this space

a group of squatters have begun moving furniture, a cooking range, portable heaters, boxes of clothing, canned pasta foods. Three men struggle with a washtub through the hallway. As one iron leg catches on a loose floorboard, they're forced to retreat and examine the remaining distance. Children scream and run up the stairs, followed by a small but loud scruffy white dog. The women hang sheets to divide the sleeping quarters. Two old men sit at a table, tapping black and red pieces on a checkerboard, arguing, punctuating their curses with spitting on the floor.

Into this space

Fellini and then Ferlinghetti lured a plump girl of nineteen who has lured three young boys who carry bottles of wine and baguettes.

The youngest drags the others' schoolbooks behind him, tied together with a simple belt. How she dances and twirls, drinks and gesticulates with the bread, now like a proud soldier with his gun, now a focused batter with his powerful bat. How the boys cheer and stamp their feet. Popping a cork, she lifts the bottle high, lifts her skirts, and smashes an empty against the brick wall. The youngest begins to cry at that, while the other two hold him back from running out. Loud whispers in his ear do still him, and he raises a new bottle high and thrusts it out to her.

Into this space

a burly seascape painter drops his easel near a wide window. Sneezing twice, he struggles with the latch, and succeeds to open the window but not without a big bang which threatens to smash the frail panes. Examining the room from different angles, he retreats, reappearing with two black suitcases, which he drags beside the easel, emptying the contents into one pile. A large blue cloth is last to emerge, which he spreads out on the floor with great care. Now naked, he lies on his back, hands clasped on his chest, eyes open, staring at the ceiling.

Into this space

a general will order his men to fire. Positions had been taken only hours before, no warning will be given, no inquiry made as to the occupants' identities or choices (whether, indeed there were occupants, and if so, were they the cause of the manoeuvre). The instructions were simple, continue firing until the building is brought down to the ground. The general is not one to question his orders; he has read the handwritten note many times over. There is no reason given, only an address, underlined with three heavy strokes of the pen, a brief statement of purpose, and an indecipherable signature the general took for the Secretary of the Interior. He was not going to take any chances either; a tank was rolled within thirty feet, two truckloads of recent recruits were dispersed in small groups to circle the building. First, the lines of communication to the building are severed. Next, traffic is rerouted, and, as the last voices of soldiers become less audible, there remains only the wait until the word is given.

Into this space

the word is given by the poet with the moustache headache, fighting off impossible demands on his flesh, and his blood type. To be known for one who "caught a glimpse of the eternal, despite clearly posted signs to the contrary" he launches one final desperate metaphor and disappears.

Into this space

you enter alone, bearing your heart, mind and body. The poem is illuminated upon the wall of your mind, it reminds you of a dream in which you were afraid and you knelt before your saviour and said I am so afraid please help and the reply was laughter and shame, you shielded your eyes with your hands and they were wet and they were bloody and you screamed and awoke in the bed of a stranger; the poem strips you bare while you're listening, the poem enters your body as an orgasm.

Paradox

John McAuley

As one becomes older
one tends to be used
by the passive voice
and the indefinite pronoun
far too much—one is even worn
by one's foils. Yet in this case
a life, mine for example,
settles in a flat cardboard box
full of oddments, contrasts, and
injustices self and other inflicted,
trifles the details over and over
until someone's hands, say yours,
pick up the box, open the lid, and
scatter the triumphant chrysanthemums.

Add This Somewhere

John McAuley

Like most didactic formless souls
I began my literary career
as an intellectual marshmallow.
The whole sorry business was all too plain,
having something to do with a turnip
that could fart with perfect ease.
I naively declared what my symbols
would be, making it easy on the dull,
but it was all slightly confusing
as I searched out a selection
of first-hand post-mortem reflections
that in no way made me religious.
For years I culled through them,
accepting man's natural right to dominate
and even championed depressingly familiar roles
for women. Well, at least that's changed.

Until my late teens, I built model aircraft:
my favourite was the cherry-red Maksim Gorkii
engineered in 1930 to blitz bourgeois standards
through leaflet drops on the masses, yet
there wasn't anything heroic about me.
I tried to divorce myself in my mind
from my allegedly helpless personas, and
discovered I didn't have any character at all.
A real zoology of manners was I, only skin deep,
not understanding that Hypnos rules
the nervous interior.

My vers libre meanderings were indolent and
inarticulate, reflecting the blunted sensibilities
of someone whose head is as empty as his stomach.
I tried to become a primitive, but
stewed on condescension and rebuff.
Holding the same conclusion then and now
might be considered tenacious, though
if I ever woke up, I think I'd die
from the excitement.

To Leo Kennedy 1983

John McAuley

The world's unbreachable ditch
waits for you to cross it where
you and I and others join
the ever-increasing tribe
whose words are their only remains.

Half a century ago and one book published,
hesitation fell to gross recklessness
frying other fish in Chicago.

Tragic success in finding your music
too easy too early,
faultless memory for the cost of each line.

Grass is greener only in rain.
Sorrows, regrets, last-hopes ditched,
posterity floating in scraps, and you
gripping your cane like a man
shaking up the moon.

Your return to Montreal rescues
no friend from the grass,
its tyranny slighting all things,
wavering no-wise,
revealing only the wind
rippling
waters in the ditch.

Northern Love

John McAuley

The stony waters of pale stars
balance on an apex of emptiness
a paradoxical edgy space.

This poem is about love's astronomical
contradictions, awkward hands of death
holding the proud above: the never-always
uncomfortable precession of equinox and
solstice. Planets seen and unseen
flutter at our passage.
Longer than any telling is
the virtue of retelling this.

Your father and mine do not reframe
their dreams, the how of death. Yet
their proof in us remains redeemed,
earthly quadrant at the cosmic core,
the dark container of fate's rotation
unassailable authority
of bones and flesh.

My Alba

Artie Gold

noted
my propensity
to trade
the henceforth for
the now. . .
(time
garbled)
(postmodernism)
which theoretically
writes off
virtually everything
for that
anything
and to me has always
seemed a good swap—but
perhaps it is time again now to
try on the world
which albeit must fit
can be nevertheless
surly
and
fit
like
a falling
piano.

Resources

Artie Gold

The freedom duplication of resources guarantees
but my one hand in your one hand when we walk...

I will be blunt; what love/
has not brought me to my knees? At least love
like some dream of plenty, mercurially gathers all into its meniscus
—shall we walk around any such granary without complete possession?

away from you
I become philosophical...
which is like taking off one's glasses *to see.*

R.W. 12

Artie Gold

My sanity as an external thing
I focus on say a twig that looks like a frog
but I want it to be just a twig
if twig it is
yet I see it always as a sort of "striving to become
a frog"
it exists
in the bubble zone. Not saying my sanity is something
in a lane I've driven by
bricked up
entombed in some uncertain back
of no, definite address, no.
I have waved to my body passing it on a freeway
and it, often, was going the other way
against me: I would feel pierced
but the world is not set up that way.
Not exactly—
the game of control is more like shaving in a mirror
or cutting hair, watching as I do the wrong thing the mirror
do the right. All through the night
I have stood, craning my neck,
my body twisting, one sun going down
bringing up another
and exhausted I have been delivered unto the morning
rather hairless, a sight.
my bald eyes sprained,
pains in my elbows where they have reached around to hold the scissors
a good feeling, another opposite
implanted in me from that harrowing night.

Acknowledgements

Photo Credits

Page 56—photos of Al Purdy and bpNichol by Stephen Morrissey; photos of bill bissett and Lionel Kearns by Karl E. Jirgens.

Page 79—photos by Stephen Morrissey and Artie Gold.

Page 83—photo by Stephen Morrissey.

Page 93—photos by David Rahn.

Page 94—"Face Off"photo by Christian Knudsen; "Close Up" photo by John Oughton.

Page 104—photo by Stephen Morrissey.

Page 114—photo by Karina LaValley.

Page 125—photos by Michel Dubreuil.

Page 128—photos by Yves Bouliane.

Page 134—photo by Christian Knudsen.

Page 137—photo by ben soo.

Page 140—photo by Michel Bonneau.

Page 144—photo of Artie Gold and Endre Farkas by Geof Isherwood; photo of John McAuley by Endre Farkas.

Page 154—photo by Susan Hamlett.

Page 156—photo by Susan Hamlett.

Special thanks to all the unacknowledged photographers and poster artists.

All poster poems from pages 58-74 are from the Poetry on the Buses project, 1979-80.

All proverbsi from *Proverbsi*, by Ken Norris and Tom Konyves, Asylum Press, 1977.

Interview with Ken Norris conducted by Sonja Skarstedt. Interviews with Tom Konyves, Endre Farkas and Stephen Morrissey conducted by Ken Norris.

Achevé d'imprimer
en novembre 1993 sur les presses
des Ateliers Graphiques Marc Veilleux Inc.
Cap-Saint-Ignace (Québec).